PRAISE FOR **THE TRUTH ABOUT PRICING**

"Before selling anything, choices have to be made about how best to price it. Most people understand the importance of proper pricing. But few recognize that there's a science to it—something that Palmer shows us clearly and impressively. Marketers would benefit greatly from this book."

—**ROBERT CIALDINI,** author of *Influence* and *Pre-Suasion*

"If you set prices for anything, you absolutely must read *The Truth About Pricing*. It will add dollars to your bottom line and wipe worry lines from your face."

—**ZOE CHANCE,** author of *Influence Is Your Superpower*

"After reading this incredible book about the psychological mechanisms that drive consumer behavior, you'll wish there was a game show called *The Price Is Wrong*, because the insights in these pages would guarantee you a chance at winning the grand prize. By offering a deeper understanding of what not to do when it comes to pricing strategies, guiding consumer behavior, and developing a relationship with your customers, Melina Palmer's guide to actionable lessons from behavioral economics will put your business ahead of the game you are already playing and help you win an even grander prize than Bob Barker could have ever offered."

—**DAVID MCRANEY,** bestselling author of multiple books, including *How Minds Change,* and host of the *You Are Not So Smart* podcast

"Small tweaks can make all the difference between a great buying experience and a lost sale. Palmer's practical insights are immediately useful to anyone wrestling with pricing."

—**NIR EYAL,** author of *Hooked: How to Build Habit-Forming Products*

"I've always felt that the trick in pricing isn't determining the dollar value, it's in how to frame and communicate the price as value. Palmer nails this trick in *The Truth About Pricing*—it's a gem!"

—**DILIP SOMAN,** director of Behavioral Economics in Action at Rotman (BEAR) and author of *The Last Mile*

"People assume that to master pricing you need to understand economics, but as Melina Palmer argues in her excellent and entertaining book, what you really need to understand is psychology. And who better to explain the psychology of pricing than Melina? With her exceptional ability to condense research-based insights into actionable advice, Melina has written the book every small business owner needs to create a pricing strategy that works."

—**VANESSA BOHNS,** professor of organizational behavior at Cornell and author of *You Have More Influence Than You Think*

"In *The Truth About Pricing*, Melina Palmer delivers an eye-opening and invaluable exploration into the complex world of pricing strategies. As a business leader who has navigated the treacherous waters of pricing for decades, I can confidently say that this book is a game-changer."

—**SCOTT JEFFREY MILLER,** WSJ bestselling author and host of the world's largest weekly leadership podcast

"In *The Truth About Pricing*, Melina takes her signature concoction of brain science, behavioral economics and psychology and applies it to the evergreen challenge of business owners everywhere: pricing. Her light, engaging voice is the perfect companion to the structured process for creating, updating, or overhauling your pricing strategy in thirty days or less."

—**KATE GIGAX,** executive coach and founder, Development Corps

"*The Truth About Pricing* reveals how the brain actually works when making decisions about the price of things we buy. Like the layers of an onion, Melina peels off the insights to help sellers solve deeper and deeper pricing conundrums in a way that is easy to read and execute."

—**JEZ GROOM,** founder and CEO of Cowry Consulting and author of *Ripple*

"This book is an actionable way to turn psychology into profit—a must-read for every entrepreneur."

—**PHILL AGNEW,** host of Nudge, the UK's #1 marketing podcast

THE
TRUTH
ABOUT
PRICING

THE TRUTH ABOUT PRICING

HOW TO APPLY BEHAVIORAL ECONOMICS SO CUSTOMERS BUY

MELINA PALMER

mango
PUBLISHING GROUP

CORAL GABLES

For permission requests, please contact the publisher at:
Mango Publishing Group
2850 S Douglas Road, 2nd Floor
Coral Gables, FL 33134 USA
info@mango.bz

For special orders, quantity sales, course adoptions and corporate sales, please email
the publisher at sales@mango.bz. For trade and wholesale sales, please contact Ingram
Publisher Services at customer.service@ingramcontent.com or +1.800.509.4887.

The Truth About Pricing: How to Apply Behavioral Economics So Customers Buy

Library of Congress Cataloging-in-Publication number: 2023945382
ISBN: (pb) 978-1-68481-343-8 (hc) 978-1-68481-344-5 (e) 978-1-68481-345-2
BISAC category code: BUS058010, BUSINESS & ECONOMICS / Sales & Selling /
Management

For Aaron, Henry, Harper, and Hudson,
who I value more than anything.

CONTENTS

THE TRUTH ABOUT PRICING

Foreword_____10

PART I: SETTING THE STAGE

Chapter 1: The Golden Octopus_____13

Chapter 2: How to Use This Book___18

Chapter 3: Pricing, Placement,
and Psychology_____28

PART II: BUILDING A FOUNDATION

Chapter 4: You_____53

Chapter 5: The Customer_____69

Chapter 6: The Market_____92

Chapter 7: The Company_____107

Chapter 8: The Offer_____119

Chapter 9: The Numbers_____128

PART III: APPLYING IT

Chapter 10: The Framework_____145

Chapter 11: The Choice_____187

Chapter 12: The Placement____217

Chapter 13: Examples_____230

Chapter 14: If You're in a Rush____249

Chapter 15: Back to You_____254

Afterword_____261

Acknowledgements_____263

About the Author_____265

Endnotes_____266

FOREWORD

CONTENTS

Pitching and selling products and services to a customer is a critical part of any business—and one full of negotiations. Some may be more explicit than others, like someone asking for a discount, but these everyday negotiations are key to every company's success. Understanding the psychological components at play and being confident in your pricing are important skills for everyone in business to master.

As the host of *Negotiate Anything*, the world's number one negotiation podcast with more than a thousand episodes, I've had the privilege of engaging with the brightest minds in negotiation and persuasion. But of all of my guests, Melina stands out. Because of her incredible insights and magnetic personality, she's one of the few who has an open invitation to come on the podcast any time she wants.

Melina's contributions are special because she consistently delivers deep insights in a uniquely accessible, friendly, and practical way. Her exceptional ability to deconstruct complex elements of psychology into digestible, actionable insights never ceases to amaze me. It's as if she has a secret decoder, translating convoluted theories into a language that anyone can comprehend and put into practice.

As the CEO of the American Negotiation Institute, I deeply enjoyed and appreciated *The Truth About Pricing*. While reading it, I was engrossed, taking fervent notes. Melina addressed some of my most pressing questions about pricing. Her book has a transformative power; simplifying a topic often filled with confusion, anxiety, and complexity. I only wish she'd written it a decade earlier! The countless mistakes and frustrations I've had with pricing over the years could have been avoided.

However, this book offers more than just invaluable insights. Melina's vibrant personality shines through the narrative, adding a layer of joy to the learning experience. You'll sense her enthusiasm and humor as you build a foundation of behavioral economics insights for your business. The book isn't just informative but genuinely enjoyable as it guides you through your new pricing strategy.

This book isn't just a business guide; it's a trek through the labyrinth of psychology in pricing. You'll unravel pricing mysteries, debunk pricing myths, and reveal pricing truths. It's a journey of discovery and learning that is as entertaining as it is enlightening. With every chapter, page, and word, you'll empower yourself, your business, and your life.

The brilliance of *The Truth About Pricing* lies not only in its expertly crafted content, but also in its execution. Each chapter presents a new facet of the journey everyone in business must go through when tackling pricing—not just the numerical aspect, but the overall experience and perception around a product or service. Using a blend of personal anecdotes, scientific research, and practical advice, Melina uncovers the layers of pricing, revealing its core: psychology. It's an approach that shifts the focus from mere economics and calculations to an understanding of the human mind and behavior—a revolutionary perspective that's both fascinating and empowering.

As a reader, what excited me most about this book is its immediate applicability. It's not just a repository of knowledge—it's a toolkit, offering techniques and strategies that can be put into practice right away. The book is a treasure trove of actionable advice that could bring a significant positive change in the way you approach pricing in your business.

Whether you're a seasoned business owner, a budding entrepreneur, or just curious about pricing dynamics, this book is a must-read. Every chapter, insight, and recommendation comes from Melina's expertise, experience, and genuine desire to help. She's penned this book with you, the reader, in mind. It's a game-changer, and I have no doubt you'll enjoy the journey.

—KWAME CHRISTIAN

CEO of American Negotiation Institute, host of *Negotiate Anything*, the #1 negotiation podcast in the world, TEDx speaker, and bestselling author of multiple books

PART I
SETTING
THE
STAGE

CHAPTER 1

THE GOLDEN OCTOPUS

In 2016, I was living in downtown Seattle with my (now) husband. Our preferred way to spend a weekend was walking through the city, popping in and out of shops while we talked about everything under the sun. My favorite place was a little home goods shop filled with exquisite, eye-catching pieces. Most were extravagant and unnecessary, including my obsession—a golden octopus statue.

Yes, you read that right.

This piece was a tantalizing blend of whimsy and elegance. Each of its eight limbs curved gracefully, shimmering under the shop's soft lighting so it almost felt as if it were moving gently beneath secret waves. It was a thing of unnecessary luxury, true, but there was something about the intricate craftsmanship, the way the metallic hue caught the light, that drew my gaze time and again. No one could ever say they "needed" this golden octopus, and while I admired it on every visit to the store, I never intended to purchase it. I don't explicitly remember having that *"Someday, I'll live a life with a house full of golden octopuses"* thought. But like the other items in the store, it was fun to admire on each visit.

My life was a whirlwind of change that year. Aaron and I got engaged. We decided to move sixty-three miles south of the city, which meant leaving a job I had been at for six years to focus on my master's program and begin consulting full-time. It was an exciting time, but things were scary too. What if I couldn't make enough money to replace my corporate income? What if I hated this town my husband grew up in and that I had only visited three times? Was I nuts?

Despite these fears lurking at the back of my brain, I embraced the opportunity and decided to jump into this new life. Our last stroll downtown as Seattleites was bittersweet. Walking and talking, we visited all our most beloved spots, and I went to bid my favorite cephalopod a final farewell.

As I admired the octopus for what I thought would be the last time, Aaron suggested I buy it to symbolize my new life as an entrepreneur. It would be a keepsake of our cherished time in Seattle and a beautiful visual reminder to inspire me to live my dreams.

My golden octopus is the first thing I bought for my office in our new home— one of the only things I still have from that time (see if you can spot it on the shelf behind me in any of my videos). This gift to my future self is one of my favorite things in our house. I always remember why I got it, how it made me feel, and what it represents.

And you know what? I have no idea how much I paid for it.

While I suggested it was "extravagant," that is more in its lack of necessity than its sticker price. After racking my brain, I think I paid less than $50 for it (clearly, it is not made of real gold). But it doesn't matter. If someone was to offer me $50, $75, or $250 (or even $1,000) for it…I don't think I would sell it. It is worth more to me than that. It symbolizes something greater—it is part of my identity now. What would I be saying about myself and this life I've built if I sold my golden octopus?

Logically, I know this is irrational, but I don't care. And it is an entirely moot point since I can't imagine anyone would offer me more than $5 for it. I know full well that one person's golden octopus is another person's, well…golden octopus. It's useless. At its full functionality, you could call it a paperweight, but in an increasingly digital world, even that is a commodity of declining value.

So, why does this matter? I mean, you came to learn about pricing, and I can't even remember what I paid for this silly thing!

Of course, that's the whole point.

THE TRUTH ABOUT PRICING

Here's the truth about pricing: **It's not about the price.**

Now, don't worry; I didn't give away the punchline before even starting the joke. I'm telling you this now because you must realize that pricing something so someone will buy it isn't about the number you choose. As you will see increasingly throughout this book, all the things that happen *before* the price—the psychology and nuance of what is happening inside your customer's brain and your own—matter much more than the price itself.

In this book you will find key insights into the science of how the human brain makes decisions, with practical advice you can use to make it easier for your customers to buy from you. Within these pages are a series of highly curated questions, prompts, and tasks you can follow as you create your overarching pricing strategy—the same ones I use with my clients. While we will get to the number eventually, there are several steps for you to complete along the way to ensure the number you *do* choose is one that lines up with the overall impression you want of your business.

This book will help you to confidently charge what you (or your products or services) are worth, in a way that makes it so people are more likely to naturally choose to do business with you (and feel better about it—often even more so than they would have when you were charging less).

Skeptical?

I get it. You may be thinking, "But Melina, I've had people tell me *explicitly* that they went with my competitor because they were less expensive." Or "I price shop all the time! *Of course*, the price matters." Or a whole host of other arguments.

When your pricing strategy isn't brain friendly—when you haven't been thoughtful enough about the skills and concepts I will show you in this book—a buying decision comes down to price because that is a buyer's last resort for making the decision. By contrast when the experience is cohesive and brain friendly, price almost becomes a non-issue. Think about it. What is something you bought that is different than what you usually buy? If you tend to be very analytical about purchases, this could be the thing you bought on a whim. These are the times when you might say, "I never do this, but why not!" or "It's such a great deal!" or "Only two left? I better act fast!"

The things I will teach you in this book will show you how making a few simple tweaks to your offer and how you present it can change everything for the better. You may not even need to change your prices or products. Sometimes, a change of wording or the order in which you bring things up can make all the difference. This book will show you how to think about the customer, the product, your company, the market, where you place it, how you talk about it, and, perhaps most importantly, how to get your mind on board with the whole process. Once you have been through this book, your brain will be unlocked and ready to tackle any pricing challenge again and again and again.

It's kind of like *The Matrix*. Once you understand the concepts of behavioral economics and how the brain works, you can't unknow them—which is wonderful. It can change all your communication for the better across your entire life and business.

That being said, it is important to note that the things in this book aren't magic. They aren't going to make people buy things they don't want or need for exorbitant prices through some sort of mind control or hypnosis (and if that is your goal, please kindly stop reading, this book isn't for you).

There is a point where even the things we want are too expensive, or their price is more than their value to us. Because of that, it is essential to know whom you are selling to and what the value point is for them (which we will talk about). This will allow you to frame your messaging in a way that makes it so the price itself becomes almost a nonfactor. You don't need everyone to buy. You need the right number of people to buy at the right price that makes sense for your business goals.

Not everyone is your client or customer. Not everyone will be able to afford what you are selling. Not everyone will want or need what you are selling. And that is okay. Knowing who you are for (and who you aren't) and in what circumstances is key as you set up your pricing strategy and consider the behavioral shifts needed to help someone choose you. I'm here to help you with that. The next chapter will give you a little more detail on what to expect from this book and who I wrote it for. Then, we jump right into my favorite topic—how the brain *really* works and what that means for your business.

CHAPTER 2

HOW TO USE THIS BOOK

I understand that many of you are eager to find straightforward, actionable advice for setting your prices. And that's exactly what this book will provide. But to achieve effective pricing, it's crucial to first go through a thoughtful process and ask essential questions related to your pricing strategy. (Hopefully, you are expecting that since you bought a book about pricing.)

The good news is that this book is expressly set up to be as close to "just telling you what to do" as it can be. Throughout this book, you will be introduced to many concepts from behavioral economics, such as cognitive biases (patterns of deviation in judgment), heuristics (mental shortcuts), and other insights. There is a lot I *could* say to you about each of them. (Most of those concepts each already have their own dedicated episode of *The Brainy Business* podcast that is thirty minutes to an hour long. Many also have dedicated chapters in my books *What Your Customer Wants and Can't Tell You* and *What Your Employees Need and Can't Tell You*, which are companions to this book. Everything you need to create a brainy pricing strategy is within this book, and those resources are available for everyone who wants to learn more and dig deeper.)

I promise to keep it as short and to the point as possible in this book. (Those who know me know that isn't my natural state!)

The goal here is to give you everything you need, in the order you need it, to help you finally get clear on your brain-friendly pricing strategy and start reaping the rewards as quickly as possible. There are citations for when you want and need to learn more, but they won't delay you from completing the task at hand. If you ever forget a term, don't worry; there is a free virtual glossary in the supplemental materials, which is found at *thebrainybusiness.com/pricing-book*. And, if you ever have a question, please ask! Find me as @thebrainybiz on social media and feel free to email me at *melina@thebrainybusiness.com* if you have a question.

WHO THIS BOOK IS FOR

You've made it this far, so hopefully you have already determined that *The Truth About Pricing* is a fit for you. For anyone who is still on the fence, I want to take a moment to outline who I wrote this book for.

The Truth About Pricing is for anyone who seeks effectiveness in their sales strategies. It serves those who want to understand their buyer's mindset and master the art of communicating value. Ultimately, this book will guide you in creating offerings that effortlessly draw people to choose you. This includes small and midsize business owners, entrepreneurs, marketers, and sales teams. It is also for intrapreneurs—those in corporations in charge of pricing, product development, sales, marketing, brand, and culture. After years of helping companies of all sizes with pricing and product placement, I know there is much uncertainty in this space, as well as a lack of practical, applicable advice people can use to confidently uplevel their pricing. That uncertainty is impacting your sales. My approach and the tips provided for you in this book have been proven time and again to help people:

- Sell more of the right stuff (what is profitable and valuable to the company as well as to customers/clients).

- Attract and retain loyal, happier clients.
- Make it easier for clients/customers to choose you and your products and/ or services without having to spend time on the phone with you or a sales team member.
- Feel excited about making sales calls, rather than dreading and avoiding them.
- Make more money and do less work.

Sound too good to be true? I promise it isn't. Stick with me, and I'll show you.

When you combine these concepts in the right way, you'll be equipped with strategies to significantly boost your sales. The lessons I will teach you in this book can be used to set up your pricing strategy for anything from candy bars to consulting services—software to shoes. Whether you work in business-to-business (B2B) or business-to-consumer (B2C); brick-and-mortar or fully online; bargain or luxury; fast-moving consumer goods (FMCG), coaching, or commercial real estate...you get the point. I have worked with it all, and these concepts still apply. *(Note: Unless something is specifically called out as being important for a service-based business, a product-based business, or something else, all the rules presented in this book apply across the board, whatever your industry or background. So, if something says "customers" and you have "clients," or if I say "product" and you are service-based, assume the words are used interchangeably for brevity and that whatever you have just read applies to you and your situation.)*

WHAT'S NEXT

Part I of this book is all about understanding the pricing problem and why properly applied behavioral economics is the key to your success. This section has just one more chapter after this one. It offers insights about the brain and outlines issues with how others talk about and approach pricing, as well as shines a light on the funny tricks your brain plays that have likely kept you stuck in the pricing trap. Letting you know how your brain is playing tricks on you is key to flipping the script and avoiding those brain tricks when they inevitably pop up—both as you work through the insights in this book and into the future.

Part II is structured into six chapters, each introducing concepts in a specific order I've curated to guide you through building a psychologically effective approach to pricing. We will not finalize your pricing number in this section of the book— that is what Part III is for. Part II includes all the important insights you need to consider to properly set up the "things that come before the price," creating a seamless buying experience for your customer (and making it so the number doesn't really matter). While other approaches tend to start big and work their way down (i.e., global market, local market, your competition, your company, the product, and finally, the customer), this book will take you on a different journey of thought. The problem with starting big is that, by the time you get to the humans buying (or not buying) what you plan to price and sell, you are too far down the path to consider what they value and how to communicate with them. The buyer is almost an afterthought in the journey. But how does that make any sense?

It doesn't, of course. But because we are a **herding** species, the most common recommendation feels like the right strategy. As you will learn in the next chapter, humans also have a **status quo bias** which makes us prefer things to be predictable and the way they are now. When someone is uncertain of what to do or where to go, they look to the herd to help them choose the right way to proceed. In the case of your customer, if you aren't the status quo and you don't know what is (and therefore aren't creating language to **nudge** them to make a new decision to buy from you) they likely won't. In the case of you as a professional setting your prices, following the herd's "big to small" approach will leave you with a very reactive strategy where you follow a leader who potentially doesn't know what they're doing any more than you do. Remember this: Just because everyone else is doing something a certain way doesn't make it right.

So, this may leave you wondering, "If we don't start from the broader market and narrow down, where should we begin?" The answer lies closer than you might think—with you. In my years of experience, I've found that one's own mindset can be the biggest hurdle to implementing a successful pricing strategy.

If you work on a team, this is the collective "you"—anyone involved with coming up with the pricing strategy or selling the product or service to your customers, clients, members, patrons, or whatever other term you use.

Why do "you" matter? When you are not fully on board and confident in your pricing, it shows. That lack of confidence will impact your buyers. I liken it to how a dog can smell fear. If you aren't confident in your pricing, the buyer picks up on the seemingly imperceptible hints that something is off. It can make it so they are more likely to ask for discounts, hesitate to buy, or even go to a competitor when they really wanted to buy from you. The wrong mindset around pricing and how you communicate it can derail everything. Establishing confidence and the *right* mindset around pricing is the most important piece of the puzzle (and the one no one else talks about). So, we start there.

Next, we turn our attention to the customer, aiming to gain a better understanding of what they truly value. Then we zoom out to the market and your competition to get a better understanding of the customer journey and what they are using now (uncovering your hidden competitors) before considering your own company. Once you have looked at your own company, it is time to choose the specific product or service you will focus on—your "**best offer**." Once you know the focus, the final chapter of this section is looking at the numbers to ensure that whatever price you choose for your best offer will be profitable and well-aligned for your business and your customers.

Once you complete your solid foundation in Part II, you are ready to move on to Applying It in Part III. This begins with my "It's Not About the Cookie" framework, which looks at six categories of behavioral science that you need to consider when applying everything you completed to create the foundation of your brainy pricing strategy. The chapter on the framework includes tips for applying each of the six categories to your strategy, showcasing how they can stand alone as well as be combined to fit any business. Next, we look at the *choice*. Including behavioral economics in your strategy provides a significant value and differentiation. One way we do this is by encouraging you to consider the 'choice architecture,' which is a crucial aspect of behavioral science. We will discuss how you are a **choice architect** and the immense value of properly structuring a choice. Most advice you see out there will skip over this, which is a huge reason many businesses struggle with pricing and sales. You will be amazed at how different everything feels when you understand and consider your customers' choice through this lens.

Once you have gone through the framework and the choice, I give you specific tips for presenting your offer in the most common scenarios, including:

- in a chart (summarizing multiple items next to each other)
- in written descriptions (usually presented stacked one on top of the other with more detail about each item, perhaps in an email pitch)
- in a verbal script (for sales pitches over the phone or in person, as well as for use in videos)

Over the years, I have found that these three tools can be applied to fit almost any situation where you need to present your pricing. They can work together or alone to give your buyer the information they need to decide. Creating all three in advance will ensure you are ready (and confident!) whenever your potential purchaser asks for more information. Having completed and polished materials ready when someone asks helps with that herding instinct we talked about earlier. The customer's thought process goes something like this: If you have everything ready, it is probably because other people have asked similar questions, and if you continue to use those items, it is probably because they work—this train of thought also makes it easier for someone to feel safe buying from you. (Whereas the opposite of, "Oh, they don't have anything ready to send? I guess they don't sell a lot... Maybe I should reconsider..." is definitely not making it easy for them to buy from you.)

To solidify what you've learned throughout the book and inspire you with what is possible, Part III closes with four case studies to get your brain buzzing on how you can apply all this to your company. Before we complete our journey together (hopefully the first of many, as this book is intended to support you again and again), we bring it back to you—remember, your mindset is the most important thing! So, the book closes with some common pitfalls and brain traps to avoid, with tips to ensure your new behavioral pricing strategy is as successful as possible.

SO, HOW LONG SHOULD IT TAKE?

How long this process takes will of course be different for everyone. If you already have a lot of research or you have a large team, it could take less time than for someone starting from scratch. Established brands will be different from new ones (though each has its benefits and difficulties). The time it takes for those with many products in a physical or online store will differ from those offering services. All this being said, the point is to make it so you don't have to keep dwelling on pricing strategy forever. No one wants that! For the brainiest approach, I recommend setting aside thirty days where you do a little bit every day. (Depending on how quickly you read and how far along you are already, I would estimate this is likely to take between one and three hours.) This will give you enough time to read, reflect, answer the questions, revisit, and do a little research where needed each day. You are of course free to approach this book however feels best to you.

When you do the work, this stuff works (and pays big dividends), I promise. One of my clients implemented my insights on bundling and went from struggling to sell an $8,000 package to having multiple new clients enthusiastically say yes to $20,000 packages. Another was able to reframe the mindset about what the company was charging and doubled the monthly average billings for a retainer client on their next call together. These are just two of the countless success stories from around the world. What will your first big success be? Please share those wins on social media using the #TruthAboutPricing hashtag so I can celebrate with you! (I'm @thebrainybiz pretty much everywhere.)

I GET IT, BUT WHAT IF I STARTED TOO LATE?

I know how often pricing can be put off for "tomorrow" or "next week" until you wake up one day and realize, "Oh no! The launch is Friday and we haven't finalized the price yet, what do we do?!" (We will talk about why this happens in the next chapter so you can be less likely to fall into this trap moving forward.) To ensure everyone who needs last-minute support has a chance to make their approach more brain friendly, I knew this book needed a streamlined option. So, for everyone who is in this kind of time crunch, there is a chapter at the end of the book called *If You're in a Rush*.

This chapter is "for emergency use only" and only exists to help you incorporate some brainy benefits to the pricing strategy at your initial launch, rather than resorting to some number you pull out of the air or that is one dollar less than your competition. This streamlined version of the process is provided with the intention that you will come back to read the full book and update your pricing strategy accordingly within six months so you and your company can have the *full* brainy benefits. Agreed?

TASK: CONNECT, SHARE, AND GET YOUR FREEBIES

Throughout the book, there are tasks for you to complete along the way. Some are areas requiring thoughtfulness, and some are a bit more in-depth. They will always have a header that begins with "Task:" to make it easy to scan back through the chapter and find them.

To show you how this works, I have created a simple task to get connected and ensure you know where your resources are. I love connecting with readers and podcast listeners from around the world, so please do connect if you are open to it! I also love questions, and, while this book will (hopefully) cover the bulk of what might be bouncing around in your brain, because it is also curated to be as streamlined as possible, it can't cover every aspect and nuance of every possible situation because...that would go on forever! Whether you have questions, want to share key insights, or would like to see what others are asking and sharing, here is how to connect:

- Tag and follow me **@thebrainybiz** pretty much everywhere (also "Melina Palmer" and "The Brainy Business" on LinkedIn)

- Follow **#TruthAboutPricing** to connect and see insights from others (and use the hashtag yourself to share insights, success stories, and anything else that has you inspired!)

- When you have a question, use **#PricingQuestion** (and also follow this hashtag if you want to see how I answer other reader questions)

In the spirit of using this book as an ongoing resource, you will notice key terms in bold as you read. Every chapter (including this one) ends with a summary box that includes a list of both the tasks and the key terms featured in that chapter.

If you are already subscribed to *The Brainy Business* podcast and/or have ready my other books (thank you!), you won't be surprised to learn that

I've created supporting materials, including a virtual glossary (in case you want to learn more about any of those key terms) as well as a Pricing Mastery checklist to help you along your journey. (Yay freebies!) Go get yours now (and bookmark the page for easy reference) using the QR code on this page or by visiting *thebrainybusiness.com/pricing-book*.

All right, you're ready! Let's dig in on pricing. And, not surprisingly, it all starts with the brain.

FROM THIS CHAPTER

Tasks:

- Connect, share, and get your freebies.

Key Terms:

- Herding
- Status Quo Bias
- Nudge
- Best Offer
- Choice Architect

Get your free Pricing Mastery checklist, virtual glossary, and other freebies using the QR code and at thebrainybusiness.com/pricing-book

CHAPTER 3

PRICING, PLACEMENT, AND PSYCHOLOGY

Since you chose to read this book (thank you!), I'm guessing you have already thought about pricing a lot. And I mean, a lot. There may have been a few sleepless nights in there—lots of stress, worry, and questions like:

- How much should I charge?

- What will people pay for this?

- Should I end my prices in a 5? 7? 9? 0? Something else?

- Will everyone laugh at me?

- What if I fail?

These questions (and a million others like them) can leave you feeling stuck. The sheer weight of this decision can be paralyzing. It feels like if you get it wrong, everything will fall apart. The result?

- After agonizing over the decision for the zillionth time, you throw your hands up and haphazardly set your price (though your confidence it was the right choice wavers constantly).

- If you are launching something new, you use this as a reason to delay and lose out on valuable opportunities (while you continue to feel stuck).

- If you have been in business for a while, you use this as a reason not to raise your prices, even though you know you are below the market or not as profitable as you should be (and, again, continue to let this question consistently linger in the back of your mind).

While I hope this doesn't resonate with you, I know this is a constant reality for far too many—especially small and midsize business owners.

Here's the good news—**you've picked the right book to stop this cycle of uncertainty, doubt, and analysis paralysis that many people experience when it comes to pricing.**

And here is some more good news: The past issues you've had with pricing are not your fault. I have helped countless people and organizations worldwide with pricing, and I can tell you this is difficult for everyone. The main lesson to know is: it's not you, it's your brain. And not just *your* brain, but all humans. Our brains are wired to succumb to the same kinds of pitfalls and tricks again and again. And while that may feel deflating, it's actually great news! If everyone does it, that makes it much more predictable, which means it can be fixed. That's what we will cover in this book.

Since the "problem" is with the brain, let's talk about that for a bit.

BRAINY BACKGROUND

In case this is our first experience together, let me take a moment to introduce myself. My name is Melina Palmer, and I'm an applied behavioral economist.

If you're unfamiliar with behavioral economics, I like to say that if traditional economics and psychology had a baby, you would have behavioral economics. Or, put another way:

Traditional Economics + Psychology = Behavioral Economics

Behavioral economics is a field rooted in science that examines how our brain—divided into two systems known as System 1 and System 2—shapes our reality and decision-making. It is the result of decades of research from multiple disciplines around the world: psychology, economics, neuroscience, and philosophy, to name a few. However, it is also an art. Hundreds of rules, concepts, and stimuli constantly work together in the brain to shape your reality and decision-making (and that of your buyers). The concepts featured in this book are proven, and we all experience them in some way every single day—and your buyers do too.

In order for this book to be most beneficial to you, I want to ensure that it provides essential knowledge without overwhelming you with excessive information. So, here are the three most important things for you to understand about the brain (to apply both to yourself as you work on the strategy and to your customers and how they buy):

1. THE BRAIN HAS TWO SYSTEMS

I touched on this a bit already, but here is a little more detail on the two systems of the brain for anyone new to the space.[1] **System 1** (which I refer to as the "subconscious" throughout my books and *The Brainy Business* podcast) is the automatic system. It is quick to react and can handle an incredible amount of information at any given time—to put it into computer terms, as much as eleven million bits of information per second.[2]

By contrast, **System 2** is what I refer to as your "conscious" brain. It is much slower and cannot handle nearly as much information. Compared to the subconscious' eleven million bits per second, the conscious brain can only do about forty bits (yikes). These two systems are both running constantly. I think of the subconscious as a gatekeeper—or the receptionist filtering through things to keep them off the desk of the busy executive (conscious).

Things tend to slow down when the executive gets involved, so the subconscious receptionist wants to hold onto as many things as it can. Is every rule and application perfect? No, but this receptionist has a "Done is better than perfect" poster on the office wall. Efficiency is the name of the game.

Subconscious (System 1) = Receptionist

Uses proven rules to make tons of quick, automatic decisions

Conscious (System 2) = Busy Executive

Can't handle nearly as much; slower, more evaluative decisions

While we like to think we're in control of our brains and all our decisions (and believe we are doing everything as a complex, logical evaluation), it simply isn't the case. The conscious brain cannot handle enough information to make the plethora of decisions needed to survive.

How many decisions? Let's play a quick game to see:

Think back to yesterday. How many decisions do you remember making?

With that in mind, how many decisions do you think you make on an average day? Twenty-five? Five hundred? Five thousand? Research has found that the average person makes 35,000 remotely conscious decisions every single day.[3] And that's not "Breathe in. Breathe out." These are actual decisions, such as what to wear, when to look at your phone, which route to take to work, and where you set down your coffee cup.

Clearly, the conscious brain isn't doing the bulk of the decision-making (think back to the number of decisions you *remember* making and compare it to the 35,000). Those subconscious decisions influence everything from which hand holds our toothbrush to which brand of toothpaste we buy to put on it, to the neighborhood we live in, the house we purchased, and the car we bought to get us there.

We know that people buy on emotion and that their process of making a decision is primarily based in the subconscious,[4] so why can't we just ask people to tap into that part of their brain and explain what they were thinking (or will think in the future)?

There's a reason my first two books have "and can't tell you" in their titles.

Unfortunately, the two systems of the brain don't speak the same language. This explains why focus groups might say they prefer a certain brand of toothpaste during discussions, but their purchasing behavior later contradicts this expressed preference. They aren't lying to you on purpose (for the most part). It turns out people don't know what they will do. And worse than that, they can't even tell you after the fact why they *did* something because the two parts of the brain aren't speaking the same language.

Want More Brainy Insights?

If you're digging on the behavioral economics insights in this chapter and want to learn more about the nuance of it all, check out my other books, *What Your Customer Wants and Can't Tell You* and *What Your Employees Need and Can't Tell You*, as well as *The Brainy Business* podcast. They dig in on all these topics in more detail than we will cover in this book (again, to leave as much space for application as possible).

Go to *thebrainybusiness.com/books* (or use the QR code below) to learn more and even read the first chapter of any of my books for free.

Use the QR code to learn more about my other books and read the first chapter of each of them for free to determine if that book is a fit for you.

The Brainy Business podcast has hundreds of episodes for you to learn from as you set up your own brainy business. Find it wherever you get your podcasts, use this handy QR code, or visit *thebrainybusiness.com/podcast.*

Most of the concepts in this book have their own dedicated episodes of The Brainy Business podcast. Use the QR code to listen and subscribe to the show.

2. THE BRAIN RUNS ON HABIT

All mammals have **habits** (whales, dogs, rats),[5] and research indicates that anywhere from 40 to 95 percent of our decisions are habitual.[6]

It makes sense when you think about it. Let's break down those 35,000 decisions people make every day. Let's generously assume you sleep eight hours per night. That means you make 2,187 decisions every hour, thirty-six per minute, or a little more than one every two seconds. Clearly, you aren't making logical, deliberate choices about each of those micro-decisions (and neither are your customers, team members, or family members).

How did you get these habits? Many of them are ingrained in us because of our evolution.[7] Fight, flight, or freeze is one of the best-known examples of how your automatic (subconscious) system responds when it feels threatened. You don't consciously evaluate what to do in those situations, and these habitual choices happen even though you don't remember learning them.

Habits can also be sequences of actions with which you have familiarized yourself over time, either by physically performing repetitive elements yourself or observing others. Think back to when you first learned to drive a car. It was likely a slow, tedious process where you were constantly second-guessing yourself. ("Where do my hands go? Which pedal is that? Don't forget to check the mirror!")

It was slow because your conscious brain had to learn and set up rules for the process. Now that those rules have been established, it's much easier—you likely didn't even need to think about any of that the last time you drove, right? That's because driving skills have moved into your subconscious brain. While you drive, your brain is still making all the same decisions and evaluations, but they are done quickly using habits.

Everything is smooth and easy—until you're driving over a mountain pass in the pouring rain between a semi-truck and a guard rail; now you feel reality shift and slow...way...down. You're aware of every tiny twitch of the wheel against your hands, every eye movement feels intense, your shoulders are raised, and you're hyper-aware.

That is the process of your subconscious handing over the wheel to your conscious brain (pun intended). Driving in this moment is too important and needs diligent focus to keep you safe. It's worthy of those forty bits per second (and something else needs to be relegated down to the level of the subconscious while driving takes precedence).

This is also why you turn the radio down while searching for a new address; the conscious brain can't handle that much input at one time. Just like when we instinctively swat away a buzzing insect before consciously realizing what it is (and then, while you know it was around before you noticed it, now it is all you can hear or seem to focus on), there are many "handoffs" happening between our conscious and subconscious minds that we're not overtly aware of.

Both types of learning—those created through the generations and via our individual experiences—influence the rules the subconscious lives by and constantly applies throughout the day. And, if you're thinking, "It sure would be great to know the rules and habits the subconscious uses to make those decisions; imagine the insight into how customers buy and want to be sold to!" I have great news. The study of these rules and habits forms the core of behavioral economics, offering vital insights into consumer decision-making processes.

3. THE BRAIN LOVES THE STATUS QUO

While I find everything about the field of behavioral economics to be interesting, this next insight is one that absolutely rocked my world when I first learned it.

Our brains are hardwired to reference past experiences when making decisions. This doesn't necessarily mean the choice will be optimal for the current situation; rather it is based on what worked well or was best in the past. This tendency, which is foundational to all of the predictability our brains need to make those 35,000 decisions every day, helps us navigate the world around us.

It is pretty obvious when you think about it, but most of us never take the time to realize this and really consider what it means. Almost everything you do in life is based on a prediction of what is coming next based on the subconscious' understanding of the past. Yes, it can be the clothes you wear and the food you choose to eat, but it is even more fundamental than that—this is why (as you will learn in this book) **micro-moments** are key to your success. As an example, in the very first episode of *The Big Bang Theory*, Sheldon tells Leonard that most people will trip if a single stair is off by as little as two millimeters.[8] While there is some debate over the exact height needed for this, a tiny difference in stair height will cause this phenomenon. See for yourself via a funny video of a particular stair in the New York City Subway that was a fraction of an inch higher than the others, causing everyone to trip (which has now been fixed—thanks, social media).[9]

But take a moment to consider *why* this happens.

Why would such a small difference matter and make people trip? It is because your brain has gotten accustomed to the height of the stairs and is telling your body what to do based on what has worked for all the other stairs you've encountered. We are wired to save energy, so you only lift your leg as high as you need to in order to get to that next stair, which causes this slight difference to catch your toe, making you stumble.

Imagine the height of a staircase you ascend every day. Your brain, in order to conserve energy, no longer consciously considers each step's height. This expected, consistent height is the status quo. But if a single step were suddenly higher, you would stumble. The unexpected change "bucking" the system throws off your brain's predictive patterns and catches you off guard.

The principle of the status quo and our tendency to rely on past experiences is not just applicable to physical movements like climbing stairs. It also significantly influences our decision-making processes in business. In situations of uncertainty, such as when creating a pricing strategy or when customers are making a purchasing decision, we tend to gravitate toward what we know. This means everyone should consider, "How is the status quo helping or hindering your business success?"

PRICING PROBLEMS

Now that we have established a baseline for how the brain works—
including its two systems, its reliance on habits, and its affinity for the
status quo, let's apply this understanding to your business. Specifically,
we will explore the three major challenges companies encounter when
working on pricing.

PROBLEM 1: TRADITIONAL PRICING ADVICE FORGETS ABOUT (OR UNDERVALUES) PSYCHOLOGY

The first issue with those pricing articles, books, and tips you may have
found in your research is that they absolutely underestimate the value
and importance of incorporating psychology into the process. Very few of
the many articles I found while researching for this book even *mentioned*
psychology. Those that did so only included it as one of the options for a
model to implement and reduced its value merely to such tactics as ending
your price with a 9 instead of a 0 (Note: this is not the best strategy for
every business, and we will talk about this in much more depth throughout
the book).

While this is part of the value that comes from incorporating psychology
into your pricing and how you position your company, brand, products, and
services—it is a tiny sliver of what behavioral economics can do for your
overarching strategy.

It is not a question of *if* you incorporate psychology (and behavioral
economics) into your pricing strategy. It is not a question of *where* you
place it, either. **When it comes to pricing and the positioning of your
products and services—psychology is everything.**

To paraphrase Michael Hallsworth of the Behavioral Insights Team, behavioral economics isn't the wrench you grab when it is time to tighten things up right before you send something out the door. It is the filter that every decision should go through.[10]

Despite our society's increasing reliance on AI, your business still involves human interactions. You're selling to humans. Those humans have brains, which they use to make decisions. Understanding how those brains like to be communicated to—and making it easier for them to choose you—will always matter. And that is what this book is all about.

PROBLEM 2: TRADITIONAL PRICING ADVICE CREATES OVERWHELM

While you were living in that stress-fueled existence before picking up this book, you probably googled something like "How to set my prices" or "Best pricing strategies" once or twice (or a hundred times). How did that go?

I'm guessing that if you finished reading those articles or guides you found, you discovered they created more questions than answers. Some have four main pricing strategies. Others list five, seven, ten, or even fourteen. The descriptions of each strategy are often filled with jargon and are either way too detailed or far too vague. The other problem is that they can only give you a bunch of definitions with very few practical tips and little applicable advice you can do something with. Giving you information about fourteen options without a clear way to choose what you should do next in your business is a perfect recipe for overwhelm and a **paradox of choice**.[11]

While we like to think that humans love lots of options and choices, it turns out that too many options can actually result in a paralyzing state where we can't decide. When creating your pricing strategy, you can end up with the scenarios I described earlier in this chapter—doing nothing or making a rushed choice you may regret.

The benefits of reducing overwhelm and too many choices also apply to buyers. For example, sales increased by 10 percent when Procter & Gamble reduced the number of SKUs for Head & Shoulders from twenty-six to fifteen. When The Golden Cat Corp. got rid of its ten worst-selling kitty litters, they got a double benefit: Their sales went up 12 percent, and, because of significantly reduced distribution costs, their profits increased 87 percent.[12]

For those who are already pricing experts, a bit of information about the dozen-plus models to choose from is helpful and makes their choice easier. For those who are *not* pricing experts...not so much. And, as you now know from the previous section about the brain, overwhelm in an unfamiliar space will increase your reliance on the status quo[13] (resulting in all of what we have been talking about so far).

PROBLEM 3: YOUR BRAIN IS FOCUSING ON THE WRONG THINGS

Because of the overwhelm and uncertainty that comes with something scary (like finally going to market or raising your prices), your brain will rebel a bit and do what it can to keep things predictable. There are a few common tricks the brain will put in your way to help maintain that status quo (i.e., that hellish state where you feel paralyzed by the overwhelm of this pricing decision). These tricks boil down to four main factors: optimism bias, planning fallacy, time discounting, and bikeshedding.

OPTIMISM BIAS AND PLANNING FALLACY

Optimism bias is what makes it so we believe that we are less likely to experience a negative event than other people. It is also one of the things that causes us to overestimate our own abilities. Whether you identify as an optimist or not, you still have an optimism bias (and the reverse is true, we all have a negativity bias as well). Optimism bias won't come up the same way in every situation, but it does impact us all on a regular basis. Classic example: Are you a better-than-average driver?

If you said (or thought), "Yes," you are in good company. Eighty-eight percent of people do, but clearly that can't be true because no more than half can be above the average.[14] And even as I say this, you are likely thinking, "Ha! All those other silly people thinking they are above average like me."

It is surprisingly hard to internalize and accept that you could very well be part of that *other* group. Stop and reflect on it for a minute. Do you believe it? Even now? (Or now?)

This optimism bias means our brains are wired to believe we are better, faster, smarter, and stronger than everyone else (including the "us" of five minutes ago). Building on that, we also have a **planning fallacy**. This is our tendency to underestimate how long it will take to complete a task, how difficult it will be, the associated costs, and the items that will distract us along the way.[15] Clearly, this is an issue for pricing strategy!

Daniel Kahneman (the first behavioral economist to win a Nobel prize) says we do this over and over because "successful execution of a plan is specific and easy to imagine," and while we focus on the few paths to things going right, we forget to account for the seemingly endless list of ways things can go awry.[16] When we don't think through how the plan can go off the rails, we will likely fall victim to planning fallacy. Frustratingly, you may have noticed that even when you have done something several times, it doesn't help you more accurately predict how long it will take next time. Right?

One study asked college students how long they thought it would take them to complete their thesis papers.[17] The average prediction was thirty-four days. They were then asked to give estimates for how that might change if everything went amazingly smoothly (in which case they predicted it would take only twenty-seven days), and also how long it would take if things went wild and there were lots of delays (for which they estimated forty-eight days).

What really happened?

It ended up taking an average of fifty-five days! This was a full week longer than the worst-case scenario prediction and three weeks beyond the original thirty-four-day estimate. Now, these students were no novices. They had written plenty of papers in the past and should, theoretically, have been able to predict the time it would take to write this one. They could have factored in "unexpected" external elements like emails, opportunities to go out with friends, boredom, the constant allure of Netflix or TikTok, and priorities for other classes. But they didn't. And that's not uncommon. Even those who missed the last deadline (and the one before that) would likely still struggle with accurate prediction.

And I know you do it too, because you are human. Whether it is term papers, work projects, high-profile construction projects, home renovation budgets, or a slew of other examples, we all do this constantly.

It is important to know that planning fallacy is more than mere procrastination. It isn't about setting better deadlines. Our brains are programmed to continue to do this even when we set up plans, are familiar with the task, have motivations or incentives to finish on time, or have planned it out with a team.[18] Frustrating, I know. But don't worry; it isn't hopeless. I've found time and again that incorporating the next two concepts—time discounting and bikeshedding—into the equation can help you understand what your brain is doing so you do it far less often. (I wish I could tell you that this will never impact you again, but as long as you're a human, this will be part of your experience.)

TIME DISCOUNTING

Time discounting is a cognitive bias where we value immediate rewards over future ones. Have you ever decided on Saturday night that you were going to buckle down and start a diet and exercise plan "on Monday"? Maybe you spent all Sunday planning and were psyched when you set your alarm that night, but felt like a completely different (and unmotivated) person when the alarm went off?

That's time discounting at work (or as I like to call it, the "I'll start Monday" effect).

Studies have shown that the brain sees our future self (whom you are committing to get up at five o'clock to run) as a completely different person.[19] It's easy to commit *Future You*, but when *Real You* faces the harsh reality of the alarm, it is easier to hit snooze (making it Future You's problem again).

Picture this: You've just launched your business, and you're constantly saying to yourself, "I'll tackle my pricing strategy when I have more customers, more time, and fewer projects on my plate." This is **optimism bias** and **time discounting** working together, keeping you firmly rooted in the **status quo** (where your subconscious is most comfortable).

How can you fight this? When you want to put something off until tomorrow, ask why.

Then follow that up with, "What can I do right now to prove to my brain this is important?" (And then...go do it right away.) The good news is that this book is set up to help you overcome these natural tendencies and is broken up into manageable chunks so you can finally tackle this in a way that leaves you feeling confident (so you can **stop dwelling and start selling**).

BIKESHEDDING

Bikeshedding, a term coined to explain the phenomenon where people spend disproportionate time on trivial matters while important ones are put aside, often makes it *feel like* you are addressing unbelievably important issues. In reality, we're just telling ourselves that we can't dedicate time to some bigger, scarier task until we solve these trivial ones. I also call this "productive procrastination," because you can work on unimportant things that make you feel like you are making progress when you are just being a hamster on a wheel.

This tendency got the name bikeshedding because it was first observed in a team that was tasked with designing a nuclear plant but spent an inordinate amount of time focused on the design of the bike shed.[20] Spending so much time on the bike shed is clearly ridiculous to an outsider. However, now that you understand that the subconscious loves predictability, it shouldn't be all that surprising.

Designing a nuclear plant is scary; there are severe consequences if you mess that up. And, until you start that project, your optimism bias might lead you to believe that you can finish it faster and more easily than is realistically possible.

Imagine that, much like the thesis-writing students mentioned, you have a new product or service in the works and must launch it in six months. Most people will get hung up on little details (i.e., bikeshed) when there is ample time. The risks of moving forward weigh heavily, and it feels like there will be plenty of time once you get that *other thing* out of the way.

In the case of pricing strategy, this shows up when you spend way too much time debating about the exact number (i.e., questions like "Should we end in a 9 or a 7?"), or reading yet another article on the different pricing models to see if there is magically a new case study that will show you exactly what to do in your situation, or mindlessly scrolling through your competitors' websites and social media accounts to see if they have changed anything since you checked five minutes ago. You continue to bikeshed because you feel uncertain about the right approach and the consequences feel dire if you get it wrong.

Then one day, you wake up and realize, "Oh no...the launch is Friday, and I've made no progress on our pricing strategy!" And, because pricing tends to come up amid other high-stress work (like a big launch, rebrand, or redesign), you pick the easiest path to checking this off your to-do list, which usually consists of picking a number just below your competition and/or one that is some simple percentage markup on your fixed costs (and then vowing that once things die down, you will come back to the pricing strategy and do it right).

Can you spot all four of our concepts in there? And, more importantly, are you ready to leave this experience behind you and finally have a pricing approach that inspires your confidence in it? One that works, and is easy? Read on, my friend.

BOOSTING THE BRAINY BENEFITS

Understanding your brain's processing can be beneficial in many ways. For anyone interested, I will provide tips on how this understanding can help you get more out of everything you learn. This will be especially useful as you go through this book and beyond, making you more likely to apply the knowledge and think about things on a deeper level. If any of these aren't your thing and/ or you already have a routine that works for you—great! There is no pressure here. My goal is just for you to be as successful as possible, so I provide best practices when I have them.

STEP 1: PREP YOUR SPACE

Begin by removing unnecessary cognitive stress and distractions. This will make a significant difference in your productivity. For example, constantly wondering, "How long has it been?" or "How much time do I have left?" drains your mental energy. To avoid this, consider strategies such as time blocking and setting alarms.

If you can, find a comfortable, clutter-free space to read and do important work like this. Why does this matter? For one thing, our eyes scan the world around us three times per second on average, so less clutter means less opportunity for distraction.[21]

TASK: CONSIDER (AND REMOVE) DISTRACTIONS

Take a moment to consider the common, off-topic thoughts that could interrupt your flow: If your mind wanders to "Should I get a snack?" and after a few minutes of internal debate you grab one, and then when you sit back down immediately realize you have to get up again because "I guess I am a little parched," then you never have enough dedicated time to get past those little distractions (bikesheds) to do the work you set out to do. Research shows it takes people an average of twenty-three minutes to regain focus after an interruption.[22] So, whatever your predictable small distractions might be (snacks, water, having a sweater in case you get cold, putting your phone on silent—and ideally in another room, making sure the kids are taken care of, closing your laptop), taking a couple of minutes to address them before you settle in can do wonders for your overall productivity and free up capacity for your brain to do deeper, more meaningful work.

STEP 2: UNCLUTTER YOUR MIND

Have you ever noticed how, once you eliminate one level of distractions, your mind immediately jumps to the next? Let's address that.

The solution: Take notes.

Yes, I know notes aren't for everyone (and as I said above, you don't have to do anything I recommend here if you don't want to), but there are some real, neuroscience-backed reasons for doing this.

If you don't get those thoughts out of your head, they can spin and spiral and take up way more space than they deserve, which results in bikeshedding. When left in your brain, all those things you plan to remember or revisit later become a great distraction, so you *feel* like you are making progress while you are never actually getting anywhere.

TASK: CHOOSE YOUR NOTE-TAKING METHOD

Whether you like to write the notes by hand, type them out, or do voice memos doesn't really matter. The point is to clear the way for more important thoughts by getting them out of your head.

As long as those easy thoughts—those bikesheds—are on the surface for you, your brain can continue to use them as camouflage from the more profound and meaningful work. So, let's get them out! Use your handy-dandy notebook (or app or whatever) to jot down all the questions that feel important when it comes to your pricing. These can get you started:

- Does it matter what my competition is doing?

- Do we need to offer payment plans?

- What about a satisfaction guarantee? What happens if everyone tries to return everything?

- Do we have to list prices on our website? If so, how do we do that?

- What happens when we sell out?

- What will my schedule be like if we sell out? Can we even handle that volume?

- Is there an ideal number of products to offer?

If any of those resonate with you (whether you were already wondering about them or not), write them down and add as many of your own as you can think of. Leave some space (a page or two) so you can write more questions as you go through the book. The good news is all the questions on this list will be answered throughout the book in due time. I'm guessing that most of what you wonder about as you read will be answered as well.

The important thing now is to get these questions out of your brain so they don't waste space. If you find yourself starting to spin on any particular question, add it to the list. If it ever resurfaces, remind yourself, "Not now. I've written it down and will work on that later."

This simple trick can help keep you focused and keep your brain in check while you work, allowing you to make real progress.

STEP 3: GET OUT OF YOUR OWN WAY

When we get into "pricing mode," something very strange happens. We almost completely forget how and why we buy. All those things we hate when we are the buyer suddenly feel like the best way to communicate. And the things that drive us to buy? We think people would hate them! This is thanks to those two systems I mentioned earlier in the chapter. But, don't worry, this is where I (and behavioral economics) come in.

Understanding our own purchasing habits can help us improve our pricing strategies. So, I recommend being more thoughtful about your own buying experiences and taking notes in the moment (or as close to it as you can) that you can reflect on later. These notes will be really helpful when you work through the steps in this book.

TASK: BECOME A CURIOUS QUESTIONER

To ensure those notes are as helpful as possible, I encourage you to be more observant—become what I call a "curious questioner." Consider the world around you with childlike wonder. Get good at asking all the questions you can. For example:

- When you see an article (or get an email) you can't help but open, ask yourself why. Were there words or images that drew you in? Was it the emojis?

- When you get an email (or LinkedIn connection request) and automatically think, *"Spam!"*—consider what made your alarm bells go off. What did they say that felt shady?

- When you buy something you normally wouldn't (your golden octopus), reflect on all the moments that led up to the purchase. What made this experience different?

- When you wrestle for ages with a buying decision that should have been easy, consider all the moments that have led you here. Why don't you feel comfortable?

How are each of those moments leveraging the concepts and tactics you are reading about in this book? How do they line up with what you have done in your communication in the past? Where are you saying something very similar to the spammy LinkedIn message? When are you making it hard for people to decide to buy from you?

Jot them all down in your notebook using your "customer" brain (subconscious mind) to revisit them as your "planning" brain (conscious mind) tries to take the reins. Save your examples somewhere if you can. I have a folder in my email called "From Others" that I can skim through when looking for good and bad messaging examples. There is another on my computer for screenshots, as well as a physical box in my office for items waiting to be photographed and stored electronically. You would be amazed by all the well-intentioned messages out there that go awry. These people and companies may be selling something fantastic that is a great deal and exactly what I need, but if the subject line feels like spam, I'll never know about it.

Alright, now that you know a little about how brains work and the tricks they play around pricing and buying, as well as tips to help you be as productive as possible as you go through the process in this book, let's jump right into building your foundation and Part II.

FROM THIS CHAPTER

Tasks:

- Consider (and remove) distractions.
- Choose your note-taking method.
- Become a curious questioner.

Key Terms:

- System 1 (subconscious) and System 2 (conscious) brain processing
- Habits
- Status Quo Bias
- Paradox of Choice
- Optimism Bias
- Planning Fallacy
- Time Discounting
- Bikeshedding

PART II

BUILDING A
FOUNDATION

CHAPTER 4

YOU

When people come to me for help with their pricing, the first question is usually something like, "How much should we charge for this?" or "What is the best way to get people to buy?"

My answer, which you will come to find is somewhat of a trademark of mine, is: "It depends."

Don't worry; I won't leave you hanging with an "it depends" and no support or direction. The next thing I typically say is, "What do you want people to do?" or "What is the best-case scenario?" or "Tell me more about your business model." In reality, you can charge whatever you want for whatever you're selling. If you position it properly, there will be a market for it at almost any price point. This is true regardless of what the competition is doing—regardless of what the existing market is. You can build a business around any model you want; properly applied behavioral economics will help you achieve it.

In the very first chapter of this book, I emphasized the truth about pricing: It isn't about the number on the tag. It's about the value, the perception, and the entire experience surrounding the product or service. Take, for instance, a designer handbag and a generic one. While their functionality may be the same, consumers pay vastly different prices for them. This is because the designer brand has been able to create a perception of luxury and exclusivity, adding a value that goes beyond the physical product. People pay all sorts of prices for all sorts of things. Even two very similar products can command vastly different prices depending on factors like brand reputation, marketing, and consumer perception. Your job is to understand the foundational aspects from this part of the book so well that your brand (and everything it stands for) is cohesive and aligned when you start to apply the concepts in Part III. This creates a smoother experience for your customer that makes it easier for them to purchase from you when they get to the pricing and buying phase.

Here's the catch: This only works if you believe it will. And that is why we are starting here before we move on to anything else. If you or anyone on your team has limiting beliefs about how much you can charge or how you "have to" approach pricing, it can keep you stuck in a nonoptimal strategy. So, to help convince the skeptics that you can charge any price for pretty much anything, here are a few examples:

GRILLED CHEESE, PLEASE

When it comes to sandwiches, a grilled cheese is about as basic as you can get. Even people who can't cook can likely whip one of these up pretty quickly at home, right? What do you think the ingredients are worth if you were going to make one of these bad boys? A dollar? And if you were going to buy one at a restaurant, what is the most you would pay for one? Five Guys has one listed on their menu right now for $4.39, so that can give some context.

Now, I want you to imagine the fanciest grilled cheese ever. Or maybe think of what it would be like if you were craving one. How much would you be willing to pay for it? What is the most outrageous price you or anyone else would pay for a grilled cheese sandwich? And, yes, you can even get fancy and assume it has a cup of tomato soup to go with it.

Now that you have your number in mind, let me introduce you to Serendipity3, a New York City restaurant with a penchant for the extravagant. In addition to the regular items on their menu, they also have a few very special items, including The Quintessential Grilled Cheese Sandwich, which costs $214.

Yes, you read that right. Two hundred and fourteen dollars. It holds a Guinness World Record as the most expensive sandwich. Serendipity3 has a few other record-holding staples on their menu, including:

- World's Most Expensive Fries: $200

- Le Burger Extravagant: $295

- Golden Opulence Sundae: $1,000

Sure, these are primarily for PR purposes, but that doesn't mean people don't buy them (nor that their mere existence doesn't support the overall brand). In 2017, when an article came out about the grilled cheese, they had already sold dozens of them. The fries were added in 2021 as a way to announce they were back open after the COVID-19 pandemic closures...and the waitlist for them at that time was eight to ten weeks.[23] For *two-hundred-dollar french fries.*

This grilled cheese sandwich is a perfect example of **anchoring** and **relativity** (two concepts from the "It's Not About the Cookie" framework we will discuss in depth in Part III), because the extravagant prices of Serendipity3's record-holders help everything else they sell feel more reasonable in comparison. This makes it so that even if their regularly priced menu items are higher than the competition, it doesn't matter. The price feels better because of these high anchors. Also, consider how many people choose to eat at the restaurant and post photos of the experience on social media (**social proof**)—even if they don't choose one of the record-holding items. The whole experience is built up by the expectation of decadence, opulence, and delight. This expectation of indulgent extravagance can lead to customers gladly paying more for the experience—and feeling happier afterward than they would have been paying less somewhere else. For example, customers at high-end restaurants often willingly pay premium prices not just for the food, but for the luxurious dining experience.

But we're not done with grilled cheese just yet! Even though Serendipity3 won a Guinness World Record for the most expensive sandwich, this isn't actually the most someone has paid for one. Do you remember the Virgin Mary Grilled Cheese?

Let me refresh your memory: A woman in Florida claimed to have been eating a grilled cheese sandwich, and that when she looked down, she recognized the face of the Virgin Mary in the bread. She promptly stopped eating, placed it in a clear box with cotton balls inside, and put it on the nightstand next to her bed for ten years. After a decade of sitting in its box (apparently, not getting a speck of mold), she posted it on eBay with a starting bid of $3,000. After thirty-eight total bids, her ten-year-old half of a sandwich (minus one bite) sold for $28,000.[24]

Of course, most people wouldn't pay that much for a *new* sandwich—let alone one that was gathering dust for a decade. But there was a market for it. Thirty-eight bids got it up to that astronomical number. While this final grilled cheese is a bit of a silly example, I hope it will drive home the point that there aren't limits on your pricing. Right now, all I want you to do is start breaking through any constraining beliefs on the upper limit (knowing, of course, that it isn't just about charging more).

TASK: CHOOSE YOUR BUSINESS TYPE

Before delving into the specifics of pricing, there's a fundamental aspect that needs to be addressed. Whether you're selling grilled cheese sandwiches or consulting packages, the first and most important decision any company needs to make is what type of business they are. And I don't mean virtual or in person, product or service, or anything like that. It is much more important to decide the essence of what your brand stands for. And while there are many terms and models which could work, I have found that in general they can be boiled down to two main paths: quality or value.

There can be all sorts of business strategies, price points, and areas of focus within each of these two categories. And the way you execute each is vastly different when we get into the process of applying behavioral economics later in this book, which is why I chose these two options.

Both "quality" and "value" are positive terms, as they both represent viable strategies. However, attempting to combine these two can lead to complications, so even if it is tempting to try and use both, it's important to pick one. This is where most businesses go wrong and what causes their pricing strategy to fail. To help you choose, let's define what makes each business type:

Quality Businesses often set higher prices than their competition, which can be due to a variety of factors. If you sell products, they may be made with higher-quality materials or be sustainably sourced. If you are selling services, your team may have expertise or special certifications that others do not hold, making you worth the additional investment. You might invest in innovative methods or extensive research and development that helps you and your customers to stand out. Luxury brands also fall into this category, so if you want to cater to celebrities or have an air of sophistication, you are a quality business as well. While the quantity you sell isn't limited per se, quality brands typically focus on making a higher margin on fewer sales. Quality brands still can talk about how they are valuable as well as how they can add value to their clients and customers. While these companies might have a sale or put things on discount, it is not part of their overall strategy and should be used sparingly with a lot of thoughtfulness. When choosing number pricing, these should be whole numbers and not rounded down (i.e., $500, not $499).

Quality brand examples include: Maserati, Chanel, Hermès, Starbucks, Apple, Patagonia, Ritz-Carlton, McKinsey & Company, Deloitte, Ruth's Chris Steakhouse, Supreme, Five Guys, Nordstrom, Verizon, Whole Foods.

Value Businesses are typically less expensive than their competition—they are a bargain, a deal, a great value for the money. They invest in efficiencies that can be passed along to their customers, members, and clients. While they don't have to sell only on quantity, they are more likely to have smaller margins and sell by volume. Value brands can still sell quality items (i.e., they don't have to be cheap or low quality). They run a lot of sales, discounts, and promotions, and these are a big part of the strategy. They reflect "bargain" pricing with numbers that are rounded down (i.e., $499, not $500).

Value brand examples include: Walmart, Costco, Dollar Shave Club, 7-Eleven, AMPM, Redfin, Best Buy, Samsung, Mint Mobile, Spirit Airlines, Ryanair, Southwest, Old Navy, Macy's, McDonald's, LegalShield, Home Depot.

Both models have merit. Both types of companies are seen across the Fortune 500. And the only way to be successful in either is to pick your path. Where companies go wrong is when they want to be high quality and also run tons of sales and discount promotions. Or if they say they are all about value but are consistently more expensive than their competition. This type of mixed messaging is confusing for your buyer, which increases their **cognitive load** and makes it more difficult for them to purchase from you. When the experience is cohesive and lines up from your first impression onward, everything becomes easier. For this reason, you have to choose a path and hold true to it throughout the entire organization.

So, you might be wondering, "Melina, why is this in the 'you' chapter and not in the 'company' chapter?" While you will see this come up again several times in the book (because it is that important), there are two reasons I have included it this early:

1. Choosing your business type is fundamental to all subsequent decisions and strategies. So, as you progress through the book, consider each task, prompt, learning, and question in the light of your chosen business type. If I waited to bring it up until you were over halfway through, you might need to do additional work, and I don't want that.

2. The biggest hurdle to holding the line on your business type and making decisions that are consistent with your chosen direction is the people in the organization. We are a **herding** species, and FOMO is real. As you look around and see other companies running sales or big discounts, you may

feel pressure to do the same. If you are a quality brand, constantly running sales and discount promotions can be a damaging strategy. It can dilute your brand's perceived value and create an expectation of regular discounts, which might harm your profit margins in the long run. If you are a value brand with some money to invest back in the organization and decide to make a flashy new logo or website with unnecessary bells and whistles (because the brand you are competing with has one), that could come back to bite you. Getting everyone on board with the business type and agreeing to hold each other accountable when the allure of another strategy looms large (it will happen) is critical to your overall success.

How much you sell something for and whether or not it is a good strategy for your business all depends on your goal. You may already know the answer to this question, or it may require some reflection, but please do choose your business type now.

I Can't Decide!

I am the queen of the pros and cons list—I can see the value in any argument (absolutely considered a career as an attorney), so I know the struggle can be real here. It can be especially challenging if your business has been doing a bit of both strategies to date, making it hard to know which one is the right path for you moving forward.

If this is you (or others across your organization), don't stress.

Take some time to imagine your business five or ten years from now—What does it look like? How much does everyone work? How do people buy from you? Do you have millions of customers or a few really invested ones? Based on your answers, choose the business type—value or quality—that is best aligned with that vision of where you want to go. As you read through the rest of Part II, continue to start with this as your default, and also take a few extra moments on each task to consider what it might look like if you were the other type of business so you can see how each resonates. (Bonus: This will also help you to create a "Do not do these things" list which you can use to identify the areas where you may be tempted to detour from your chosen path later on.)

Part III kicks off with this same task—to solidify your company type. This will be a final opportunity to reflect on what you learned throughout Part II and determine if your initial plan was the right one or if you want to switch. Either way, you will be set up for success when it comes time to apply the framework.

TWO QUICK CASE STUDIES

To help firm up your decision, this section includes two short case studies—one quality brand and one value brand. Like the Serendipity3 example earlier in this chapter, they each include bolded terms, which are key concepts in the "It's Not About the Cookie" framework that kicks off Part III. Because we are digging deeper into these concepts later on in the book, I do not define them too extensively here—just enough for you to understand the context. They are called out because I want them to be on your radar, and this will serve as a good reference point if you ever flip back to these examples later. Remember, each term is included in the virtual glossary if you need it.

QUALITY: SUPREME

If you've never heard of the streetwear brand Supreme, get ready to question everything you thought you knew about business, pricing, and brand strategy. They have a fascinating model which revolves around extreme **scarcity**. Most weeks, typically on Monday, they announce what is being dropped that week. At eleven o'clock New York time on Thursday, the drop happens, and once everything sells out a few minutes later…you'll never see them again.

Well, you'll never see them at *retail* again, which already has a huge markup on what the same (or very similar) items would go for without the Supreme logo. One of the countless examples is the Pyrex two-cup measuring cup. A regular one of these can be purchased for less than $5. Those with a Supreme logo retailed for $24 when they dropped in 2019. That in itself is amazing when you think about it. The logo is the same red as the print on the cup, so it is pretty hard to see—if you weren't looking for it, you might miss it—yet people happily paid five times as much for the same readily available measuring cups with no functional difference.

Supreme has partnered with all sorts of brands over the years, including Louis Vuitton, The North Face, Fender, Nike, Dr. Martens, Everlast, Hanes, Lacoste, Burberry, Levi's, the New York Metro, Spalding, Timberland, Vans, Honda—even Oreo. Nearly anything you can think of (and many things you never would) like crowbars, toothpicks, fire extinguishers, dominoes, dog bowls, and even a brick with the Supreme logo on it that retailed for $30—all sold out.[25]

Extreme **scarcity** and high demand mean a massive resale market for anything with the Supreme logo. Those Pyrex measuring cups? At the time of this writing in 2023, one is listed online for $137 and another for $250. The clay bricks? Those sold for as much as $1,000 on the open market. Yes, for a clay brick. Supreme's most expensive resold item (so far) was a Louis Vuitton trunk which went for $125,000 at a Christie's auction.[26]

Your lesson: You don't have to follow the **herd** and do what everyone else is doing, or follow the standard industry advice for anything. Just because everyone does it one way doesn't mean it is the best way, the right way, or the only way. Supreme is unapologetically expensive, and they don't chase after their customers. They play hard to get, and people pay to be part of the in-crowd.

VALUE: COSTCO

While it's common for companies to look for ways to charge more to increase profits, that isn't the only helpful strategy. Take Costco, for example. If you are a member of Costco, you know and trust that they have invested in finding high-quality items, which they provide at the best possible price. This trust makes it so many shoppers don't even take the time to compare against other retailers. If you see it at Costco, it is best to buy it, because, whatever it is, it probably won't be there later (this is thanks to their own fantastic **scarcity** model, which is different than Supreme and still incredibly effective).

One specific way Costco proves their dedication to saving members money is their hot and ready food (**reciprocity**). Whether it is the $1.50 hot dog and soda combo (which has been the same price since 1985)[27] or the $4.99 rotisserie chicken (which are the same price as they were when they launched over twenty years ago),[28] you know that Costco cares about their members, their wallets, and their full stomachs.

How popular are these meal deals? Costco reportedly sold 151 million hot dog combos in 2019[29] and 117 million rotisserie chickens in 2022. How much do they make off them? When you look at them in a silo, Costco loses massive amounts of money by keeping those prices fixed even as their expenses go up. On the chickens alone, Costco said they *lose $30 to $40 million per year* in gross margin by keeping them at $4.99.[30]

So, why in the world do they sell them so cheap?

Lots of reasons. For one, they encourage people to shop more often, and most people don't just grab a chicken and leave (since they are strategically located at the back of the store, you have to walk past all the other good deals and free samples—more **reciprocity**—on your way in and out). Another reason is because of the positive press they generate. People post and rave about the brand and its dedication to keeping prices low, which leverages **social proof** in a way that is so much more effective than if the brand tried to shout about itself.

How Would You Measure That in Pies?

While I was working on the episode of *The Brainy Business* podcast on the behavioral economics of Costco,[31] a friend told me, "All I know is, it only takes five pumpkin pies to justify your membership." Whether you calculate the value in rotisserie chickens, hot dog deals, or pies...Costco is full of great deals for fans to make TikTok and YouTube videos about.

Your Lesson: Whether you think about it in advance or not, the prices you charge say something about your business and what it stands for. Costco's commitment to great values on some key items echoes across the entire brand. Clearly, not all of the four thousand SKUs at Costco are losing them money as they had a net income of $5.8 billion in 2023.[32] They have strategically chosen some items that keep people coming back in a way that helps increase profits across the company. That being said, having a "loss leader" just because it has worked for other companies (but without understanding what it is going to do for your business) is a bad strategy. Likewise, looking at each product or service in a silo and ensuring it is profitable on its own without consideration for the overall brand and portfolio is *also* a bad strategy. Taking the time up front to be thoughtful about what your brand stands for, its goals, and how that aligns with what your customers value is critical for your pricing strategy (and is what we will work on together in the coming chapters).

TASK: REFRAME LIMITING BELIEFS

There are countless other examples where companies have seen incredible success by choosing a model different from that of the competition. And know that the mental hurdle you need to overcome isn't just about raising or lowering the price of something—it could be changing your industry's entire model. When something hasn't been done in your space before, it can feel scary, but recognize that you are in good company. Many of your favorite business cases—Netflix, Amazon, Zappos, Airbnb, eBay, and Peloton—are just a handful of the many companies that have proven breaking from the herd can be successful and profitable. I'm not saying you need to change an industry, but you don't need to feel limited by its assumptions, either.

Think of your favorite brands—how did they stand out from the crowd by doing something different? How does their pricing strategy support that initiative? When have you felt the pricing was out of alignment with what you believed a brand was about? How did that impact your buying experience?

The main lesson from this chapter is to get out of your own way—to remove your own limiting beliefs on what can be done, what has been done, or how things have to be.

- When you find yourself thinking, "No one would ever pay more than $XX for this," remind yourself of the instances where customers have paid astronomical amounts for seemingly ordinary items—like $200 for fries, $1,000 for a brick, or $28,000 for a grilled cheese. This serves to illustrate the potential of a well-executed pricing strategy.

- When someone on the team (the collective you) says, "We *have to* do it this way," remember how Supreme and countless other brands have shown us that just because everyone else is doing it one way doesn't make it the only way, the right way, or the best way.

- When you think, "Everyone else is raising their prices, so we must as well," consider your full model, company type, and pricing strategy and remember Costco. You don't have to have the same approach as everyone else to win.

Framing (and, in this case, reframing) is one of my favorite concepts in behavioral economics. In its simplest form, it finds that *how* you say something matters much more than *what* you say. Even the slightest change in how you say or think something can have a massive impact on the outcome. Yes, we will talk about framing again when we get to positioning and sharing your product or service with potential buyers, but for now, it is key to unlocking your pricing confidence.

Here's what you do to reframe your brain:

Day 1:

- Take thirty minutes to write out all your preconceived notions and beliefs about pricing strategies, trends in your industry, and existing business procedures or operations. These are what I call your "known truths"—the things everyone would agree are true at face value and never question.

- And, yes, I mean it when I say thirty minutes. I know you think you can get this done in five or ten, but it is important to get past the surface-level stuff and dig a little deeper into the subconscious brain. You will hit a wall and feel like you have listed everything possible at some point. This is when I say to my clients, "Write at least ten more..." Get them all out, write them quickly, don't second-guess. Just get them out of your head, and don't try to solve anything yet.

- After thirty minutes (or longer if needed), put the list away for the day.

Day 2:

- Pull your list back out and read through what you wrote the day before. Take another fifteen minutes to add to the list. Don't worry about repeats. Again, just get it all out.

- Go through the list and reframe each item as a question you could ask yourself or a statement that can help you realize that it isn't necessarily true. Then provide an example from the real world that proves the known truth/ limiting belief wrong. The following table shows an example of what this could look like:

KNOWN TRUTH	REFRAME IT	PROOF THAT'S WRONG
"No one would ever pay more than $XX for this."	"What would make people value this so much the price didn't matter?"	Supreme Pyrex measuring cup, brick, and countless other items
"People only buy this way."	"Is that just because people have only sold it that way? What if we couldn't do it that way anymore?"	Peloton's membership approach; Netflix; Amazon; Airbnb
"Everything needs to make money for us to be profitable."	"What other value is this item providing?"	Costco rotisserie chicken, pies, and hot dog deals

While completing this task or others recommended throughout this book, you may encounter moments of doubt where the task might not seem important. Or you may think that you "basically" know all that stuff. Or that you'll do it tomorrow or next week. Be mindful of the **status quo** trap your brain constantly sets for you via **optimism bias**, **planning fallacy**, **time discounting**, and **bikeshedding**. This trap happens when we overvalue the way things currently are (the status quo) and undervalue new possibilities. If optimizing your pricing strategy is important to you and your business, I encourage you to continue pushing through those moments (another opportunity for a mental reframe!) and complete the tasks as they've been laid out. Every step of the process is designed to help you achieve your business goals.

FROM THIS CHAPTER

Tasks:

- Choose your business type.
- Reframe limiting beliefs.

Key Terms:

- Anchoring
- Relativity
- Social Proof
- Quality Business
- Value Business
- Cognitive Load
- Reciprocity
- Scarcity
- Herding
- Framing
- Status Quo Bias
- Optimism Bias
- Planning Fallacy
- Time Discounting
- Bikeshedding

CHAPTER 5

THE CUSTOMER

Now that you see the unlimited possibilities for your pricing strategy, it is time to narrow down who it is for. Whether you have customers, members, clients, or something else, and whether you are selling directly to consumers or are selling to businesses (i.e., B2C or B2B), you need to consider who you are selling to and what they value.

In the previous chapter, we explored the concept of **framing**—the idea that how you say something matters much more than what you are saying. A slight change in your wording can significantly alter your outlook and the perception of your customers. Framing your message properly is one of the most important aspects in the "It's Not About the Cookie" framework. The insights into your ideal customers from this section are the foundation for ensuring you properly frame your pricing and placement when the time comes.

I know this will not be the first time you hear that you need to get specific with your messaging, your target market, and who your product, service, and/or brand are for. I also know that this is a lot easier said than done. It's another one of those funny brain tricks where you consciously know what you *should* do, but when the time comes to implement—you just can't seem to find the logic in making it happen. One contributing factor to this challenge is the psychological concept of **loss aversion**. This is a lot like FOMO, or "fear of missing out." This term encapsulates our innate fear of losing our chance to get or experience something, which can lead us to avoid making specific, narrowed decisions.

It probably won't surprise you to learn that humans hate to lose things. In the context of business, this can mean customers might hesitate to switch products or services due to the fear of losing what they already have. This concept is crucial when considering your pricing strategy. Studies have found time and again that people are twice as likely to be motivated by a loss than a gain.[33] And, as you now know, when you are in unfamiliar territory, your brain is more likely to rely on these subconscious tendencies. That means when it's time to commit to a narrowed scope or to niche down…you suddenly see nothing but the potential lost opportunities. The what-ifs creep in, and your brain's loss aversion alarm bells start going off. You might say or think things like:

- "But our product can help anyone! We shouldn't deprive them of the opportunity."

- "What about the backlash we might get from the markets we don't cater to?"

- "More potential customers have to be good, right?"

- "I know other companies have needed to narrow down, but…our company is different."

Just like when you chose your company type in the last chapter, it is important to resist the temptation to give in to these thoughts. Do you see how they are a tactic by your brain to keep you in the status quo?

GENERALITIES AREN'T RELATABLE

Here's the brainy reason why you need to push through the mental block that you're a good fit for everyone and pick a specific customer you are talking to: Humans need to feel emotion to make a decision, and anything generic isn't going to evoke those emotions.[34] A great story can make all the difference. Consider the Significant Objects Project. They bought random items at flea markets and thrift stores for less than $3.00 each, hired professional writers to give each item a fictional backstory, and then posted them for sale. They included the author's byline to let people know the story was not real. What happened? By giving each item a unique, compelling backstory, the Significant Objects Project was able to appeal to a specific group of buyers. As a result, the hundred items they paid a total of $128.74 for garnered $3,612.51 on eBay.[35] That includes a figurine bought for $3.00 and sold for $193.50 (a 6,333 percent increase)[36] and a cow vase whose monetary value had a 3,000 percent increase when it went up from the $2.00 it cost to the $62.00 it sold for.[37] These unique stories appealed to a specific clientele, but much like my golden octopus, they wouldn't appeal to everyone. Getting specific means you exclude some people, and that is okay. More than okay, it's typically required.

When you try to cater to "everyone," your story, messaging, and branding become too vague. Customers can't see their unique needs and values reflected in your story, and therefore lack the motivation to act or engage with your product or service. They have their own status quo bias to contend with.

Getting someone to buy means you must be enticing enough to overcome the status quo. For example, by highlighting unique features or exceptional service, you could convince a customer that your product is worth changing their habits or spending a bit more. It is your job to make whatever you are proposing appealing enough that their subconscious wants it more than it wants their current situation.

The way to do this is by showcasing the right stories. So, how do you find yours?

If you have an existing brand, company, and customer base, you have a treasure trove of information to dive into. If you have previously conducted research in this area, reviewing those findings would be an excellent place to start. While quantitative and qualitative research are both helpful, when you are looking for stories and trying to understand the subconscious brain of your customer, qualitative is going to be your go-to. Ideally, you want to find things that are in the customer's own words: sharing about their pain points, what they love, why they chose you, where they use you...whatever you can find. Even if you haven't conducted formal market research, you can still learn a lot from the spontaneous feedback you receive. For instance, keep an eye on what people are organically saying about your brand on social media and online reviews as they are great resources for unfiltered feedback. And depending on the site, many of the profiles people use will have public information about other items they like, don't like, or have bought in the past. Digging a little deeper can help you gain lots of insights about your customers and what they care about. And don't limit yourself to the items you think are directly related to your company, product, or industry. Your ideal customer is a complex web, and it is worth the effort to understand as much of the nuance of that web as you can.

When you decide whom to focus on, take some time to get outside of your own status quo bias. Just because a particular demographic was your focus in the past doesn't mean they are the right target for you moving forward. As you consider which customers will be the best fit for your business in the future, know that it isn't just about spending the most. Remember those customers who are providing high value in other ways, such as repeat purchases, high engagement levels, or brand advocacy. This is your opportunity to look to the future and shape who you want to focus on moving forward. When you look at who is buying from you now, who are the top customers you love working with? Those people who make you say, "If we could just get ten more clients like Anne, things would be great!" Gather all those best clients and see what makes them special. What do they have in common? What makes them different from the rest of your clients? Similarly, who are the customers you know are taking up a lot of time, money, and energy to serve? What do *they* have in common, and how is it different from the new focus area? These insights can help guide your strategy later on.

If you are launching something new, you need to do this as more of a thought experiment, but there is still plenty of information out there. In many ways, this is ideal because you aren't anchored on an existing and outdated customer base that can trigger that FOMO mindset. You can focus on anyone!

Whether you are coming from an existing company or starting a new venture, it is better to get as specific as you can. You can always broaden the market later when the time comes, but for now, you need to learn everything about the specific target customer and what makes them tick.

PREPARE LIKE A GREAT ACTOR

Think about your favorite actors, the ones who transcend the screen and get you lost in the story. What makes them so different from mediocre actors or regular people? Preparation. Method acting is a process by which an actor essentially becomes the character, and many go to great extremes to achieve the right mindset, mannerisms, and emotional connection. Consider Daniel Day-Lewis, who refused to wear a modern winter coat while filming *Gangs of New York* and came down with pneumonia as a result. Or Meryl Streep, who completely isolated herself from the rest of the cast during the filming of *The Devil Wears Prada*. These actors immersed themselves until they deeply understood their characters' motivations, struggles, and environments—similar to how you must understand your customers' wants, needs, and contexts.

To get into character and understand the motivation, stressors, and breaking points, method actors need to know as much as possible about what it is like to *be* that person *in* that situation.

In most cases, you (and most people in your company) are not your customer. You are not the target market. As an example, those who are naturally good at marketing have a hard time understanding how difficult it is for others to complete their marketing tasks. If a marketing company prices their services based on how much they would be willing to pay for someone to do that same work for them, they are likely to underprice.

And this problem extends beyond creating the product or service. Even if you are just selling it and didn't create it, you have likely gotten too close and know too much about the product or service to truly understand where the customer is coming from. This can be a real problem when it comes to pricing strategy, because, often, you wouldn't pay the price that it makes sense to charge for whatever it is you're selling because it doesn't align with your own individual value points! Getting out of your own way and understanding the value you create for the customer is key to knowing how to price whatever you are selling.

Once you know the customer on a deeper level, it is much easier to communicate in a way that will motivate them and make it so they instantly know that whatever you are selling is the perfect fit for them. Just like the method actor who prepares intensely to embody a character, your deep exploration of your target customer may seem intense. However, this understanding will be integral in shaping all subsequent decisions about pricing, marketing, and even product development. The good news is that the insight you gain here throughout Part II will help you to shape all your messaging and ensure it aligns with that ideal client in Part III. Every aspect of your communication, from the text on your website to how you present your offers, stems from understanding who your customer is and what they value, which should also align with the type of company you are. The scripts for your sales staff, storyboards for fifteen-second ads, and even a four-word headline for a social media post should align with this understanding.

ALL THE QUESTIONS

What should you know about your customer? Ideally, as much as possible. This section provides a non-exhaustive list of potentially valuable insights. While going through the list, you will notice some interesting questions like, "If they were a drink at Starbucks, what would they be and why?" Questions like this are there to help tap into your subconscious brain and uncover hidden aspects of the multifaceted personality of that consumer. We humans are complex beyond anything imaginable. So, if you only ask basic demographic questions like "How old are they?" "Are they married?" and "What is their household income?" you will still end up with vague information that doesn't help you create a compelling story. Yes, you still need to ask those things, but you can't stop there.

To illustrate how easy it is to misinterpret demographic information, consider this common example often shared online. Let's say you determine your target customer:

- Is male
- Was born in 1948
- Has two kids
- Has been married twice
- Grew up in England
- Likes dogs
- Is wealthy
- Lives in a castle
- Is famous
- Vacations in the Alps

This is a very specific list, right? You likely believe you did your homework and reached a clear target customer. It turns out you could be talking about both/either: Ozzy Osbourne or King Charles. These are two people who pretty much anyone would say are complete opposites and yet have all those things in common. So, while you might be tempted to skip the "random" stuff, know that it matters and is there for a reason.

Making the Case for "Random" Questions

Once while doing this type of research for a client, one of the questions we asked staff and their customers was, "If the company was a car, what type of car would they be and why?" One of the company's owners said, "A Porsche Cayenne, because we are high-end and built for performance." Yet customers often described the company as "a beat-up old truck, because you can depend on them." Traditional questions like, "Are you satisfied with our services?" and "Do you enjoy working with us?" might not have gotten to this more profound insight, but such a disconnect is significant when positioning your brand, products, services, and price.

My client's task was to decide if they wanted to reframe their opinions about who they were to match how their customers saw them, or if they needed to reposition their messaging so customers saw them how they wanted to be seen (i.e., making that company type super clear so it aligns with the ideal customer—the situation they found themselves in was an issue of saying they were "quality" while putting out lots of conflicting "value" vibes). Relating to something that seems random (like the make and model of a car) can unlock the brain in a way more obvious questions don't.

TASK: UNDERSTAND YOUR IDEAL CUSTOMER

Take some time to answer each of these questions in as much detail as you can. Resist the temptation to rely on assumptions wherever possible. As you saw in the sidebar above, what you think people should say or should want isn't always accurate. As mentioned, this isn't an exhaustive list, but rather a compilation of questions I have found to be effective over time.

What magazines do they read? Where do they hang out? Do they have kids? Are they married? How old are they? What terms do they use (slang or otherwise)? What music do they like? What is their favorite social media channel? If they were a car, what make and model would they be and why? If they were a Starbucks order, what would they be and why? If they were an animal, what would they be and why? What makes them laugh? What makes them uncomfortable? What do they find annoying, and what is their pet peeve? What is their favorite type of music? What gets them super excited? What other brands do they love? (Are they part of the BeyHive? A Harry Potter fanatic? A die-hard football fan? A Harley rider?) What do they value? What do they not value? What do they hate? Where do they like to go on vacation? What makes them nostalgic?

You can ask many questions here, and you should expand on this list. Ask and answer questions that are related to the industry you are in (for example, if you sell investment services or work in tourism, you should understand where they like to go on vacation, and there may be different sub-questions that tie in with that which are relevant to you). Also, ask questions you think have nothing to do with your industry. Humans are messy and can't turn off the things you may think are unrelated to their decision to do business with you. Understanding the "tribes" they belong to and those aspects of their identity can help you find relatable turns of phrase, case studies, partner organizations, and so much more.[38]

TASK: UNDERSTAND THE EXPERIENCE

When you consider your product/service/offering—where does this fall in the overall experience that the customer is undertaking? Don't just think about the stuff they do with you, like once they see your ad or walk into your store, but the journey they are on when they encounter whatever problem you are solving for them. People buy things and take action to relieve pain points. Something happened to trigger that pain point—what was it? Why were they doing whatever it was? What outcome do they want? What outcome do they need? Who would they call (or what would they do) today to solve this issue if it isn't working with you? What is their status quo (i.e., what happens if they do nothing)?

If you're wondering where and how you could pinpoint a journey of a person who isn't you and who you (potentially) can't talk to, I recommend that you start by thinking about where most people find you. You should have already identified where your customers "hang out" and their preferred social channel. Whether it's YouTube, LinkedIn, a podcast, TikTok, or anything else, this is the first step in their journey. This is where most of your ideal customers will find you. Now you can start to ask questions like:

What did they do before this? What do you want them to do after? What would come next? What is the ideal journey a customer is on, or the perfect customer life cycle? If you don't resolve the full problem, what alternatives might they resort to (or combine with your offering)? Are there any new problems created by working with you? What might they be? What are the gaps in their current experience? What would make them hesitant to buy? What problems have they had with other providers in the past? What questions might they need answered before they feel comfortable buying? What is solving this problem worth to them? And once they find you...what happens next?

Awareness is essential, but it doesn't mean much if people don't do anything. This is also why I don't put much stock in high circulation numbers or big follower counts and subscriber figures—if the people aren't engaged and aren't *your people*, it will still be a waste of money. Remember those **micro-moments** and the 35,000 decisions people make each day. You need to be compelling enough in the micro to get them to act. Think about breaking down the journey in these small steps (instead of giant leaps).

It would be great to say, "We did a TikTok, millions of people saw it, and everyone bought!" (Giant leap.) Unfortunately, it doesn't really happen that way. Instead of beginning and ending with you (i.e., you made a video and posted it and you don't consider anything else until they make a purchase), get curious about all the small steps in between—the micro-moments—to get from post to purchase. That looks a little more like this:

You post a video to your Instagram. People see it—some of them like it. A few even share it. You are consistently creating content they like, so they follow you. They peruse your profile. They scroll down the page a few times and then back up to the top. They watch a few stories or reels. They glance at the description. It's easy to read. An emoji catches their eye. They decide to do some investigating and eventually land on your website. They find your products/services. Those are listed in a way that makes it easy to decipher the best option. They learn more. They scroll. Click some more. Put things in a cart. And finally, buy.

Now, when we look at the truly "micro" moments, I have cut out a lot of steps here for the sake of brevity because I'm guessing you get the idea.

Each of those moments is potentially **nudgeable**—an opportunity to keep them moving along by making that path clear and enticing to stay on. In this journey, something like **social proof** can be leveraged over and over again to keep nudging the customer along. For example:

- How many likes, comments, and shares your video has on Instagram
- How many followers you have when they check out your profile
- Reviews, star ratings, and testimonials on your website
- A "Most Popular!" tag on the item you want them to buy

- Pop-ups on your site that say, "Suzie Q. in Kalamazoo just bought this same thing"

- A "Sold Out" message across multiple items or a "Restocked" message

It's vital to consider all aspects of your customer's journey; they're important to fully understand the customer experience. I invite you to take some time now to list out your micro-moments—and don't forget about the moments that happen *after* they buy. After all, most companies don't want to put in all the work to get someone to buy and then never interact with them again. Repeat business is important, and customers have lifelong journeys with brands. When you think you have all your moments listed, see if you can add seven more. When you first start doing this, it is hard to get "micro" enough, so drilling down and dividing your steps up once you think you are "done" is a great way to push yourself into identifying your true micro-moments. Once you have your list, use my Nudgeability Quadrant to prioritize them. The quadrant has two aspects: importance and nudgeability. By plotting your points on the quadrant, you can identify which moments to start with as you begin to incorporate **choice architecture** in Part III. Don't worry about that yet, right now all I want you to do is to list out your micro-moments, plot them on the Nudgeability Quadrant (example to follow), and keep that handy.

Is It Nudgeable?

A moment is "nudgeable" when you can introduce a behavioral economics concept and it is most likely to influence the choice someone makes in that micro-moment. For example, let's say you have a subscriber model for your business. Because keeping existing customers is generally more profitable than acquiring new ones, you want to keep customers from leaving (also known as lowering your attrition rate). Once someone has canceled their account, getting them to buy from you again is really hard, and a simple nudge likely isn't going to do the trick. (This is why it is more expensive to reacquire these types of customers.) There are many moments *before* they cancel that could be more nudgeable and reduce their likelihood of leaving, and those have varying levels of importance along the customer journey. If they ever call in to customer service or send a complaint email, that is a very important moment, and one that is likely full of nudgeability (this means it will fall somewhere in the top right section of the Nudgeability Quadrant). While sending the bill is also nudgeable, it is likely less important than the customer service call (it will show up lower on the importance and possibly more to the left than the previous point in the quadrant). Each micro-moment gets a point on the quadrant based on how nudgeable and how important it is.

The term NUDGES is an acronym for the six types of nudges: iNcentives, Understand mapping, Defaults, Give feedback, Expect error, and Structure complex choices.[39]

In this context, let's specifically focus on the "D," "G," and "E" aspects of NUDGES: Defaults, Giving feedback, and Expecting error. Consider these factors in the following sequence:

- First, you should ask what you want the person to do in this moment. What is the action you want them to take? Is it to click to learn more? To schedule a call? To visit your website?

- The **default** is essentially your status quo: What happens if potential buyers do nothing? What are their existing rules, habits, and heuristics (methods they use to simplify making decisions) set up to have them do in this moment? If you don't nudge them, what is the most likely course of action?

- Next, ask yourself where they might mess up: This is the **expect error** phase. Look for all the things that are keeping them from taking the desired action you identified. Where might they get distracted? What happens if they click the wrong button?

- That is now an opportunity to **give feedback** to nudge them back onto the right path. As an example of how this works, car manufacturers expect that you may make an error from time to time and forget to put on your seatbelt (something you probably want to do). If this ever happens, there is a dinging noise that gets progressively more annoying (giving you feedback on your error—a nudge) until you change your behavior. If everything had a ding, ping, or flashing light in your car, you would ignore everything, so they needed to prioritize what is most important (i.e., most likely to save your life) and only allow those top things to give feedback.

My Nudgeability Quadrant is a valuable tool to prioritize moments where a nudge could make a significant difference. You plot your moments on the quadrant based on their potential impact and the likelihood that someone can be nudged in that moment. The more important something is, the higher it goes from top to bottom. The more fixed a behavior is, the further it goes toward the left-hand side, and those that are more nudgeable are toward the right. The image on the next page shows you what the Nudgeability Quadrant looks like so you can use it to prioritize your nudgeable moments:

MELINA'S NUDGEABILITY QUADRANT

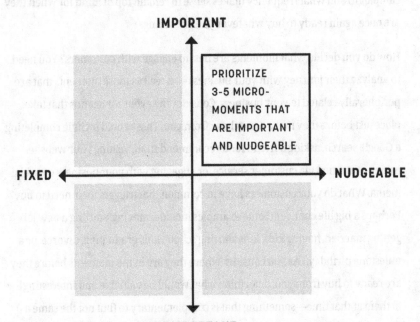

IMPORTANT

PRIORITIZE
3-5 MICRO-
MOMENTS THAT
ARE IMPORTANT
AND NUDGEABLE

FIXED ◄————————► NUDGEABLE

UNIMPORTANT

Plot your micro-moments on the Nudgeability Quadrant to prioritize where to focus your choice architecture initiatives.

Once your moments are plotted on the quadrant, identify three to five that are the most important and the most **nudgeable**. Make a note of these for future reference as you will revisit them throughout the book.

TASK: STAY ON THEIR RADAR

Every business needs to remain on the radar of their current and potential customers. While you are thinking about their journey and experience now, take some time to consider some ways you could connect with your customers between purchases (i.e., newsletter, social media, direct mail, advertising campaign) and what frequency makes sense to remain top of mind for when they are once again ready to buy whatever you are selling.

How do you decide what moments are best to engage with customers? You need to analyze their journey with your business—as well as those moments that are peripherally related to your business. Consider the events or actions that take place just before they make a purchase from you. These could include completing a Google search, asking a friend for a recommendation, visiting your website, asking a question via customer service, or engaging with your business on social media. What do your customers have in common that triggers their need to buy? Perhaps a big life change? (Some examples include: moving, starting a new job, getting married, having kids, kids starting school, kids graduating, divorce, or a milestone birthday.) As you consider where they are in the moments before they are ready to buy from you, determine what would be valuable and interesting to them at that time—something that is complementary to (but not the same as) what you charge money for. Once you know what that valuable and timely tidbit is, give it away for the low price of an email address (**reciprocity**).

Why do you want to get email addresses?

Email addresses allow you to communicate directly with your audience. It's a more personalized form of communication and less dependent on third-party platforms. If you rely solely on social media platforms, you are at the mercy of their algorithms and policies. With email addresses, you have direct and more reliable access to your audience.

Once you get someone to join the list, you also need them to *stay* on the list, so be thoughtful about what you send them and how often they receive it. There are far too many boring newsletters out there that no one wants to read, and one of those won't do you any good. Your goal is to create something they want to receive and are excited to engage with. If you want some inspiration, check out the *Why We Buy* newsletter by Katelyn Bourgoin and hear her talk about the strategy behind her highly successful content marketing approach in episode 201 of *The Brainy Business* podcast.[40]

In addition to that conversation with Katelyn, I have dedicated two full episodes of *The Brainy Business* podcast to lead magnets,[41] so I won't get into this too much more here. That being said, I do want to leave you with three tips around where I see most people getting this wrong:

- Whatever you think you need to create is probably much bigger than necessary. Go for something that will give your potential client a quick win.

- Underpromise and overdeliver. Give your new subscriber a bonus tip or something that will provide a little **surprise and delight**. This will help them associate you with a positive experience.

- Choose a frequency that matches your sales cycle. For example, if you're a real estate agency, a monthly newsletter might be appropriate given the length of the home buying process. That being said, you might also have a "hot homes" list that people can subscribe to when they are ready to get serious about moving. This list could be sent much more frequently—daily or even a couple of times a day—so the subscribers can be first to know about new listings. This is a win-win approach because your potential clients get an edge they need to secure a home in a competitive market, making you a trusted resource. In addition, your agents have a hot leads list, which can make their time prospecting much more efficient. Whatever frequency you choose, *be consistent*. Pick something you can stick to so people can rely on receiving your communication. You can't become a **habit** if they don't anticipate and get excited about hearing from you.

Make some notes about what your lead magnets could be (i.e., a workbook, a checklist, a quiz, a sample report, an e-book, a special image, bonus content, and countless other things), how they work in your customer journey, and how often you will communicate with whatever method you select.

DO I HAVE TO HAVE A FREE OFFER, SUCH AS A COMPLIMENTARY SAMPLE OR TRIAL PERIOD?

No, you don't. While this is a strategy many brands employ, it's not a requirement, and every brand has the freedom to choose if they want to give anything away for free. I like such offers as an option to help encourage people to sign up for an email list, but they don't need to be giving away anything extra for free to be worth subscribing to. For many people, being "in the know" about their favorite brands could be enough to want to be on the list. Knowing when your favorite brand is releasing a new color or style or doing a drop gives a benefit that is worth the trade of an email address as well. No matter what you sell or what is common practice in your industry, you are never required to do anything for free. Take the time to consider what your brand is about, what a free offer would mean for you, and how that aligns with your brand type (quality or value) and the items you will be selling, then determine if it is right for you. Whatever you choose, you still likely need some way to interact with your customers, so consider what that looks like and how you will maintain those relationships over time.

IS THAT THE SAME AS A LOSS LEADER?

No, a loss leader is a little bit different than a lead magnet. A loss leader is something you do at a steep discount (or even for free) as a first step in the process because you know the likelihood of someone doing more business with you afterward is much higher, making it worth the investment up front that costs you money.

For example, if you are a landscape architect, you may give away the design plan for free or do one for $99, even though it costs you at least $1,000 worth of time to create it. This is a good investment if you know that most people who get the plan are going to invest in the project, which costs $30,000 on average. If you can get ten people to agree to a free (or $99) design plan and six of them buy, you now have $180,000 in revenue (and "lost" $4,000 on the plans that didn't convert—yet). If your likelihood of getting someone to agree to have a plan created for $1,000 is four (instead of the ten plans), and two of them convert, you end up with $64,000 in projects and fees. Even if they all converted, you would only have $124,000 in projects and fees, so using the "loss leader" approach would likely have been worth it.

Of course, this approach doesn't work for every business, but it can be applied to both quality and value businesses. You need to consider what your goals are, your conversion ratios, how fierce your competition is, the time the loss leader takes to create, and more to determine if this is a good fit for you.

And, if you're wondering why presenting a plan would increase the likelihood of securing a deal, it relates to **loss aversion**. As a reminder, this principle states that people are more motivated to avoid a loss than to achieve an equivalent gain. By presenting a plan, the customer already feels a sense of ownership, and thus a loss if they choose not to proceed. When we can see and experience something (or if you have an opportunity for people to touch the product), it significantly increases the likelihood that their brain will claim ownership over it and want to buy it. It is one thing to explain what the yard might look like when it is done, but seeing it as a rendering and realizing how much better it is than that same yard today can make it hard to resist. If you've ever watched HGTV or any other design network, you know what this is like!

TASK: FIND STORIES AND ASK FOR TESTIMONIALS

Social proof—the idea that people's decisions are influenced by what others are doing—is a powerful tool in marketing. If potential customers see that people like them are satisfied with your product or service, they are more likely to make a purchase themselves. Therefore, it's important to find the relatable stories that are within your existing client base. You need to ask for ratings and reviews, create case studies, and gather testimonials.

DON'T WAIT UNTIL YOU NEED THEM

If you wait until the time when you need testimonials to ask for them, you are more likely to **bikeshed** and never get the important task done, so get in the habit of asking for them before you need them. Enlist the whole team to look for and gather great stories that align with your brand focus. Create a consistent place and an easy process for everyone on your team to follow so they are easily accessible when it is time to use them. Make asking for testimonials a standard part of your process, because you never know when you will need that great story (and bonus—you might uncover hidden pain points that you can fix to make it easier for everyone to do business with you—a real win).

INTERVIEWING TIPS

If you decide to conduct some interviews, ask lots of open-ended questions and avoid leading them in any particular direction. **Framing** matters here as well. Saying, "So, you have been struggling with your current software system. Tell me about that..." will get you to a very different place than saying, "Tell me about a typical day at work." And then when they mention the software system, you can say, "Tell me more about that," and "What is that like?" And add, "What would make your job easier?"

People often feel compelled to fill periods of silence during conversations. In an interview situation, this can work to your advantage. If you ask a question and then allow a period of silence, the interviewee may provide more depth or detail in their answer to fill the quiet. So, resist the urge to immediately jump in with more questions or comments, and instead give your interviewee the space to elaborate. Aim for three to five seconds of pause. Count it out in your head; even though it will feel like an eternity, bear in mind that is kinda the point! Your face should have a look that is kindly encouraging them to continue, and hopefully that will compel them to keep talking and dig deeper into whatever they are talking about (or sometimes, go off on a random tangent that may be very telling). Depending on the goals of the interview, I also like to ask questions like, "What would make you excited?" or "What would make you love it?" It is also common to ask, "If you could wave a magic wand and fix everything, what would be on the list?" or "If money were no object, what would you do first?" or "If you randomly got an extra $20,000, what would you use it for?"

Brainy Tip: Record any interviews you do, capturing both audio and video if you can, as there is much you can learn from facial expressions and body language. This will allow you to actively listen while they speak and ask better questions. Don't try to take copious and comprehensive notes because you will miss key things they are saying (not always with words) if you are focusing on writing or typing it all in the moment.

TASK: STAY CURIOUS

Whether you're learning about your customers through your own observations or via interviews, you might wonder, "When have we learned enough about the customer?" The truth is, there's always more to discover. Insights can quickly become outdated, so maintaining a frame of mind of constant curiosity is vital for understanding your customers. This is why having a "curious questioner" mindset is so important.

It's not enough to just establish an initial understanding of your customer—you have to maintain it. Humans are ever-changing, after all. So, I recommend you create a recurring time on the calendar so this doesn't fall through the cracks. This can be done weekly (in which case, I recommend asking five to ten new questions in that session) or daily (in which case, try to add at least one or two per day). This can be assigned to multiple team members via a centralized list (because different people on your team have diverse perspectives, so they might ask different questions and/or get different responses than you would). This will help your customer to be a living idea instead of something that sits collecting dust on a shelf and is forgotten. Keeping the customer's needs and values top of mind is imperative, ensuring they continue to be central to your strategy and will therefore continue to buy from you even as their language, experiences, and backstory may change over time.

And if you ever wonder, "Does this insight matter? Should I even write this down?" The answer is yes.

You need a good place to store that information so it doesn't become overwhelming, but any insight you can gain into your customer's mind can be helpful and is worth noting.

Brainy Tip: Especially if you have multiple team members contributing answers to an ongoing repository of information, have a way to make notes on who contributed the thoughts, and encourage each person to include a little bit about *why* they provided a specific answer. What seems intuitive in one moment could baffle in the next (or to a different person). So having some notes that can jog the memory (and a note of who to even ask to learn more when there are questions) will save a lot of guesswork, running around, and lost insights down the road. It is also a good idea to have regular conversations with the team about new customer insights—quarterly or twice a year is fine. But this practice can help ensure everyone continues to be on the same page and understands who the customer is and what they value. This can also help identify gaps in your understanding of the customer so you will have some idea of what to ask and discover next.

FROM THIS CHAPTER

Tasks:

- Understand your ideal customer.
- Understand the experience.
- Stay on their radar.
- Find stories and ask for testimonials.
- Stay curious.

Key Terms:

- Framing
- Loss Aversion
- Status Quo Bias
- Micro-Moments
- Nudge / Nudgeability Quadrant / Nudgeable
- Social Proof
- Default
- Habit
- Expect Error
- Give Feedback
- Surprise and Delight
- Reciprocity
- Bikeshedding

CHAPTER 6

THE MARKET

By now, you should understand your customer, their values, and their challenges. The next step is to research the existing market, including your competition, to correctly position and price your product.

Why does understanding your competition matter? Even if your product or service is completely unique, the key to positioning it correctly lies in comprehending your customer's current choices and **habits**.

Seen this way, even completely innovative products and industries still have competitors. If your customer is currently handling the task themselves or using another solution in a different industry, that's your competition. Your challenge? Persuade them to abandon their current choice for your offer.

Regardless of how appealing or superior your new option is, this doesn't necessarily mean customers will act on it.

Remember, people are naturally wired to prefer what they're currently doing—the **status quo**. They are drawn to what is familiar to them (**familiarity bias**). The brain's default choice is to continue its current course. This holds even when the existing path is inefficient or objectively "bad." Changing their behavior is often the last resort.

How do you break the cycle and get someone to buy? How do you persuade someone to abandon their default choice (your competition) and instead opt for your offer? The answer lies in their habits.

HABITUAL BUYING

You already know that the human brain runs on habit, but what does that really mean? And how can an understanding of habits help you evaluate your competition and when to be most appealing to your customers? Start by taking a look at your own daily routine as an example: Everything from checking your phone first thing in the morning to your mid-afternoon snack choice is built on habits. Understanding these subconscious patterns can help you anticipate your customer's needs and preferences, including why they buy (or don't).

When we think about habits, we tend to only think of the bad ones—those habits we want to break and set New Year's resolutions around—but everyone has a plethora of personal and professional habits they rely on every day. Remember those 35,000 daily decisions? We couldn't manage them without lots and lots of habits.

So, what exactly is a habit, and how does it form? Habit expert Wendy Wood defines it simply as a mental shortcut that we develop over time. This shortcut is created when we repeatedly perform actions that consistently yield some kind of reward. When she joined me on *The Brainy Business* podcast, she also provided a very simple way to know if the thing you are doing is a habit. If you can be thinking about something else while you are doing it—it's a habit.[42] (As a fascinating thought experiment, consider this: If you are writing an email or reading a text while participating in a Zoom meeting—which is the habit?)

HOW HABITS WORK

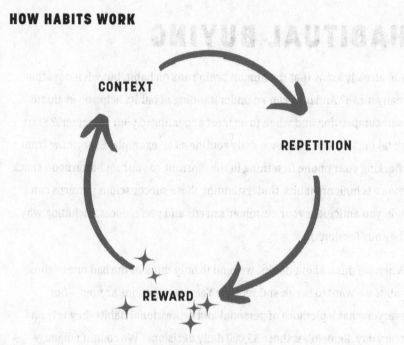

How habits really work.

As you look to identify your customers' habits (your next task), brain chemicals are a very important motivator to be aware of. Our brains constantly seek feel-good chemicals like dopamine, oxytocin, serotonin, and endorphins (sometimes referred to as the **DOSE brain chemicals**).[43]

- **Dopamine is tied to anticipation**. If you order a pizza and are waiting for it to be delivered...and then waiting for it to cool down before you grab a slice...and then raising that slice to your lips as you prepare for the first bite...your brain is releasing dopamine all along the way. The release of this feel-good chemical stops once you actually eat the food. Because any business can leverage dopamine and the value in building anticipation, this is the most common brain chemical relationship I recommend companies to focus on.

- **Oxytocin comes from connection, empathy, and trust**, so it is another chemical that is really important for any type of company. Research has found that a great story that pulls us in—even via video—can trigger the release of oxytocin.[44] This is another reason why it is important to understand your customer journey and tell compelling stories that build trust and connection. It increases the likelihood they will feel comfortable buying from you.

- **Serotonin is related to confidence, social status, and belief in your own abilities**. So, if your brand is able to help people feel like they have status (possibly through something like gamification, or showing follower counts and likes), that is a good way to help them build you into their habits.

- **Endorphins are the body's natural pain reliever**. The most commonly relatable experience of the release of endorphins is the "runner's high." So, focusing on endorphins and their habits could be a good strategy for personal trainers or those offering a thrilling experience (like skydiving, mountain climbing, or other sports).

These aren't the only chemicals or processes going on in the brain, of course, but they are a great place to start when your business is considering the buying habits of your current and potential customers—both to see where you fit and where you need to put in some effort. And, don't worry, for your level of application, you don't need to know exact measurements of the chemicals being released or anything like that. Instead, this exercise is to understand the motivation and look for moments to incorporate feel-good chemical-releasing moments into your experience. These are items that the conscious often thinks we would "hate" but the subconscious really loves—another of those funny brain tricks.

Remember, habits form when the brain establishes patterns to gain predictable rewards, which is why repetition is crucial.

Over time, the brain associates an action with its context—the location, companions, and time, as well as sensory inputs such as sights, sounds, and smells. Eventually, that context makes it so the behavior automatically comes to mind, and the cycle continues, reinforcing itself again and again.

Let's use a personal example to illustrate this concept. My go-to indulgence is chai tea lattes. They're delicious and sugar-rich, which my brain craves. Once it is a daily indulgence, it is expected and becomes a hard habit to break. Driving past Starbucks on my way to work, I may tell myself to be strong. "You're better than this, Melina. Do not touch the turn signal!" I give myself logical pep talks and try to rely on willpower. My eyes glance at the clock: I've got time, and I *need* a latte today (but this is the last time, I swear!). Tomorrow I'll start my new life when I have less on my plate, but today I've already turned into the drive-thru.

Trying to will myself not to stop when my brain is already excited and knows it could get some reliable rewards is extremely difficult (making willpower a terrible strategy for changing habits). If you want to disrupt your customer's current process so they now choose *you* instead of whatever they usually do, you need to understand the context and rewards so you modify the right things.

In my case, something as simple as taking a different route to work so I don't drive past Starbucks (changing the context) eliminates the cue (seeing the logo) and can change the habit.

TASK: IDENTIFY CUSTOMER HABITS

Don't worry; you don't need to know *all* the habits, that would be impossible and take way too long. Instead, you are looking for critical habits along the buying journey to uncover your competition and when, where, and why the customer will be most open to your offer.

Since you are looking at a new pricing strategy and potentially a brand-new offering, we are going to assume that you aren't the current habit. In the chai tea latte example, you aren't Starbucks. Whether you are a rival coffee company, or you sell chai tea latte flavored protein powder, or are a nutritionist, a personal trainer, a financial planner, or a whole host of other things, you can see why understanding this habit and where you fit into the equation is important in the buying journey.

As long as your potential customer is content with their routine chai, they might not be sufficiently interested in exploring alternatives and changing their behavior. Which moments (and corresponding habits) you need to pay attention to in the customer journey will change depending on what you are selling. The financial planner, personal trainer, nutritionist, rival coffee company, and protein powder brand might all care about the chai tea latte habit, but for different reasons. The financial planner is looking for opportunities to get small wins in the bank account that can add up (as well as how their wisdom and insight may make the customer want to invest with *them* instead of somewhere else). The personal trainer or nutritionist may be interested in the money the customer is spending that could go to their services instead (and in using this messaging to help justify the cost), and also need to know what might derail the client's opportunity for long-term health success.

Remember the list of **micro-moments** and the **Nudgeability Quadrant** you created in the last chapter? Those resources are a great place to start as you consider the habits of your ideal customer. You have already thought about their journey, so take some time now to consider the cues and brain chemicals that may be at play. What is the recurring context that lets them know there is a reward waiting?

Once you have identified the habit, the next question is, when would they be most open to your message? Here is an example of the chart with two different moments of habit from a nutritionist's point of view:

HABIT AND CHEMICALS	CONTEXTUAL CUES	WHY IT MATTERS FOR US	WHERE WE MIGHT FIT IN
Daily chai tea latte (dopamine)	Drive by Starbucks each day	A lot of people say they don't have enough money to pay for a nutritionist. The $150 they are spending each month on coffee is a great place to start and is a good spot to cut calories.	Once they are in line, it is too late (not very **nudgeable**), so we need to message before and/or after. Maybe a radio ad or some geofenced ads near the Starbucks?
Scrolling through Instagram (dopamine, serotonin)	Bored, tired, notification on phone	When people crave distraction, they often also crave sugar or fatty food; this is a time they might fail.	Better Instagram and TikTok presence. Use the common hashtags for bad food to come up in the scroll at the right moment.

As you've experienced with the "customer" chapter, your goal here is to be thoughtful about as many angles as you can. You won't end up using them all, but investing the time is important so you don't just scratch the surface and do the easy ones—your competition will have done that already. To stand out and be relevant in the perfect moment, so that you are the clear choice and the price isn't really an issue, you need to invest in the process. It will get easier as you practice, I promise.

Once you have compiled your list of customer habits, **identify the top five** instances, habits, and opportunities that you think will be most crucial as you plan your next steps.

THE POWER OF THE RIGHT MESSAGE AT THE RIGHT MOMENT

Dan Gingiss, author of *The Experience Maker*, was a guest on *The Brainy Business* podcast. In our conversation, he shared a touching story of a father whose son was undergoing surgery at Children's National Hospital.[45] At any age, your child having surgery is scary. Watching your kid go through something so difficult is a stressful time of overwhelm. And, as Dan shared, this dad felt the need to be the rock for his family. After a long day, he stopped to use the restroom and realized it was his first moment alone to reflect on his emotions from the day. While washing his hands, he looked up and saw a sign in the mirror that said, "Hang in there, Dad."

This man was immensely impressed by his experience and felt compelled to share his story. He expressed his amazement that someone had taken the time to understand his situation and deliver exactly the right message at the perfect moment.

Yes, at that moment, the parents had already chosen their hospital, and hopefully, they wouldn't have to be back again. But think about how this can put a bright spot in what would otherwise be an awful experience. When they have a choice of where to take their kids in the future if a need should ever arise, do you think they will even question going back to Children's National Hospital? When someone they know is scared because they found out their child needs surgery, who will they recommend?

I chose this example because it shows how even in industries where we don't think of "selling" to a "customer," investing in the right moments and understanding your clientele can significantly impact their future decisions. Consider the value of one loyal patient to a hospital. It's huge! Especially compared to a sign on a mirror. People often trust the words of fellow customers more than the entity itself—resulting in **social proof**. That's why delivering great experiences is crucial—they inspire word-of-mouth recommendations.

Whatever your industry or experience, take some time to consider all those micro-moments. As you can see from this example, even routine trips to the bathroom could be an opportunity to have a huge impact. The thoughtfulness you put in now will make you that much more ready to apply everything in Part III.

TASK: IDENTIFY THE COMPETITION AND POTENTIAL PARTNERS

Now that you have your list of critical moments, your customers' underlying habits, and where you might come into the equation, it is time to evaluate your top five moments and consider who the competition is at those points.

Yes, the obvious competitors should go on there. Your direct competitors are the obvious ones; if you were the nutritionist in our example, these would be other nutritionists in your area. However, consider indirect competition too. Think about the different ways potential clients could distract themselves or get nutritional advice from other sources. These could be social media influencers, wellness apps, or even Starbucks if you are competing for limited financial resources. And don't forget boredom reducers, which are competing for your client's cognitive bandwidth and capacity to feel like they can put in the effort to cook, or go shop for healthy food. These could include social media apps like Instagram, TikTok, and YouTube, or games like *Fortnite* and *Candy Crush*.

Take each of your top five moments and consider them one at a time. Really take a moment to step back from the obvious and list out at least five competitors for each moment. No more than two can be direct (obvious) competitors. Even if you aren't sure if someone or something counts as a competitor, write it down. Going back to the brainy note-taking tips from Part I, getting the surface-level stuff out of your brain and onto a page will allow you to dig deeper and find more interesting insights.

Context is so important, and much like the message on the mirror at the children's hospital, your timing matters when you want to resonate with your customer in the perfect moment. I know a wellness coach who helps her clients to change their relationship with food. She knows that Thursday night is a time where a lot of clients may fall off the wagon (i.e., revert to old habits), so that is when she sends a motivational message or releases a tip video on her YouTube channel to help keep them on track. The same message wouldn't have the same impact on Friday morning or Monday at lunchtime. Understanding the customer journey helps her to be supportive at the right moment and leads to her being seen as a true expert and ally, which makes it easier to buy from her (or continue to use her services).

Brainy Tip: During this research, make a habit of saving links to your competitors' websites. Don't limit yourself to just the top five. Also, note down key details such as their pricing model. Doing so now saves you work later. Whenever a new competitor enters the market, add them to the spreadsheet so they don't get forgotten when you revisit your strategy later.

COMPETITION	WEBSITE	PRICING MODEL	OTHER NOTES
ABC Nutrition	www. abcnutrition.com	Subscription for $XX a month, or one-offs at $XXX per visit	Been in business for five years, niche focus on people with autoimmune diseases

And, of course, the market isn't only about competition. While you conduct your research, consider where there might be overlap with the "competition" that would allow you to work *together* instead of against each other. When you look at the full journey your customer is going through, you will not be able to solve every problem they have along the way. They will need other resources and to buy other products or services to help alleviate their pain points. Where might you set up a referral relationship with someone else on the journey?

For example, someone who has just been to the doctor and been told they need to make healthier eating choices will likely consider working with a nutritionist. They can be left to their own devices and whatever Google suggests, of course. But they are much more likely to value advice from their doctor (**social proof** and **authority bias**), especially in that crucial moment. Imagine if the doctor says, "There are several nutritionists in the area. However, other clients like you have found a lot of success with Melina's Nutrition. Here's their number and website so you can book an appointment." Such a referral becomes a compelling recommendation for the potential client. This scenario is more valuable for you at Melina's Nutrition than merely hoping your company will appear in a Google search. Bonus: This also makes it so **familiarity bias** works in your favor when you *do* show up in their Google search later and they recognize your name. It is also more affordable since you didn't have to pay for ads (or it increases the value of any ads you do invest in). And, once again, when they have that recommendation from someone they trust (social proof), it becomes less about price.

Brainy Tip: Because we humans like to give back when someone has given something to us, the best way to encourage someone to make referrals to you is to *give referrals to them first*. This is known as **reciprocity**. And even if you don't start by giving those referrals, don't just go into the other business and ask them to do something for *you*. Lead with what you will do for *them* and see what they might offer to do in return. For example, you could go to the doctor's office and say, "Hi, Dr. So-and-so! Sometimes I have clients who are showing warning signs of diabetes, and I am looking for a trusted partner I can refer them to for testing and support. Is that something you would be interested in? If so, do you have any materials you would like me to provide them?" Have some of your materials in a bag in case they ask, but if they don't, be patient. You can ask for their support on a future check-in.

TASK: IDENTIFY TIMELINES AND MILESTONES

There is one last thing I want you to consider about the market before we move to your company: Is there seasonality for your offering or any critical timelines or milestones in your customer's life that you should keep in mind? For example, due to the **fresh start effect**, we like to take on new tasks and feel more motivated at the beginning of a week, month, or year (hello, resolutions!) and on milestone birthdays.[46] It may not surprise you to learn that people are much more likely to run their first marathon / half marathon / 10k / 5k when they are an age that ends with a nine (29, 39, 49, 59) versus a year that ends with a one (31, 41, 51, 61). If you are a nutritionist, it would be helpful to know who has a milestone birthday coming up so you can message them when they are most interested (i.e., at 39 instead of 40 or 41), as well as considering those major life events that come up (i.e., high school reunions) that are likely not lined up with a decade but are still important for this type of business.

Whatever your offer is, the fresh start effect can be significant when considering motivation and the right time to message your potential customers (as well as what to say at each moment). Just as the different days of the week impacted the mindset of the wellness coach clients I mentioned earlier, the message your company sends on the thirtieth of the month may be different than on the tenth.

When is payday? Are there any relevant holidays where people will be most interested in buying from you? How far in advance should you communicate about those things? Are you available year-round or only at those special moments? Are there resources that are limited in availability, either specifically within your own business or more generally across the entire market? If so, what are they, and how can their **scarcity** be leveraged as a valuable aspect? And, of course, what is the competition offering to fill these moments right now? Where are there gaps in the market?

KitKat in Japan

To illustrate the importance of understanding your customer and their context, let's consider a fascinating example shared by Matt Johnson and Tessa Misiaszek in *Branding That Means Business*, which involves KitKat's sales in Japan. After about three decades of unremarkable sales, the team noticed that sales spiked from December to February each year on the island of Kyushu.[47] After some investigation, they realized that within the Kyushu dialect, "KitKat" sounded much like the phrase *kitto katsu,* which translates to, "You'll surely win."

Students were organically giving KitKat bars to others as good luck charms around exam time, a tradition that led to the spike in sales.

KitKat in Japan went all in on these insights, knowing that they should align their messaging with exams and other milestone moments to boost sales when people were already looking for them (leveraging habits). Understanding the importance of symbolism in culture, they even included cherry blossoms—a symbol of good fortune—in their advertisements. This is very different from KitKat's global "Gimme a Break" messaging, but it made sense for Nestlé in this regional context. This goes to show why it is so important to be a curious questioner and continually dig deeper on all the psychological aspects in this book that others may say aren't related to buying behavior. It all matters. One tiny insight can change everything, if you take the time to find and understand it.

What about other happenings that will gain national or international news? These could be related to sports, politics, weather, school schedules, concert tours by your customers' favorite artists, or anything else. Make notes and keep track of any important dates. If you have any internal timelines, launch dates, or milestones coming up, these should also go on the list.

Now that you know what the market looks like, let's dig in on your company and where it lives within that market.

FROM THIS CHAPTER

Tasks:

- Identify customer habits.
- Identify the competition and potential partners.
- Identify timelines and milestones.

Key Terms:

- Status Quo Bias
- Familiarity Bias
- Habits
- DOSE Brain Chemicals (Dopamine, Oxytocin, Serotonin, Endorphins)
- Micro-Moments
- Nudge / Nudgeable / Nudgeability Quadrant
- Social Proof
- Authority Bias
- Reciprocity
- Fresh Start Effect
- Scarcity

CHAPTER 7

THE COMPANY

In this chapter, we delve into the essence of your company—your mission, values, brand, and pricing strategy. We'll discuss the power of brand consistency that aligns with your company type (**quality** or **value**), the impact it has on your customers' decision-making process, and how your pricing strategy ties into it. This chapter will guide you through the process of defining your brand and why this is crucial to your pricing strategy. The good news is, I am guessing this will be the easiest chapter for you to complete, as it is the most likely to be supported by existing documentation and materials. Companies of all sizes invest in creating mission statements, vision statements, corporate values, brand promises and standards, and other documents to help tell themselves and the world who they are. All those background documents are great and helpful when working on your pricing strategy. Gather them together and take some time to read through what already exists. Yes, at least skim through everything. Whenever I start working with a new client on pricing, I tell them to send me everything they have, and I review it all. You never know where the gems might hide in old marketing materials, annual reports, previous advertisements, and scripts.

In this chapter, you will do similar work to what you did in the "you" chapter where you tackled **loss aversion** to feel good about narrowing your focus. The areas of focus for your company include: revisiting the type of company you are, making decisions about your model, determining whether or not you will offer discounts, and considering the value of a satisfaction guarantee.

But first, we have to talk about the importance of a great brand.

Unlike a mere business which primarily focuses on selling products or services, a brand transcends that to establish a deeper, more emotional connection with consumers. Our favorite brands become part of our identities.[48] Consider this for yourself: What are some of your favorite brands?

Whatever came to mind for you, I'm guessing you didn't see numbers on a spreadsheet or a cost/benefit analysis. Of course not. Maybe you saw the Apple logo, could almost taste (and instantly crave) your favorite Starbucks Frappuccino, felt the thrill of your first family trip to Disneyland, or could smell the leather seats in your Volvo.

Whether we're building relationships with brands or with people or developing our own identities, we often base our actions and decisions on past experiences. According to *Psychology Today*, "Like a character made of LEGOs, we're built of blocks of memory that all fit together to form our consciousness."[49] And so, not surprisingly, as Peter Steidl says in his book *Neurobranding*, brands are memories, too.[50]

Now let's talk about a vital aspect of your brand identity—your value statement. This statement, which encapsulates your core beliefs and what you aim to project when customers see your logo or hear your name, matters because it establishes consistency in your brand. If you don't have a consistent brand message and promise, your vibes will be jumbled. This is why you must choose the path of value or quality and stick with it. If you don't, your potential customer will be left with extra **cognitive pressure** as they process the conflicting information. When there isn't a precise alignment, it is harder for them to make the buying decision because there aren't enough reinforced messages to form that clear memory. It's like your LEGO bricks are in a big jumble on the floor, and you are asking them to imagine it as something really cool (I promise!) instead of being built into something awe-inspiring that sticks in their mind. Great brands stick with us and form new associations in the brain.

In one study,[51] students primed with the flash of a logo during a video (only thirty milliseconds, so the conscious brain couldn't realize it even happened) were more creative in their tasks when shown the Apple logo than the IBM logo. Similarly, those who saw a Disney logo were much more honest in the subsequent tests than those who saw the logo for E!

Is that amazing, or what?

The first thing I want you to realize is how dedicated those brands have had to be to have that kind of impact after thirty milliseconds of exposure to their logo. That is some powerful stuff! **If your customer got a flash of your logo and it could only mean one thing to them, what would you want it to be?** Whatever that one thing is—everything needs to be working to help build that memory. And that naturally includes your prices.

Here the brand logo is what we refer to as a **prime** in behavioral economics. **Priming** is another of the concepts in the "It's Not About the Cookie" framework, which we will get into more in that chapter. For now, the simplest definition is to know that what happens just before a decision (word choice, images, etc.) has a big impact on the decision someone makes. When someone was primed with the Apple logo, their behavior changed to emulate what that brand image meant to them: creativity and innovation. The prime of the IBM logo did not have the same impact.

Just think about Costco, which we covered earlier in the book. Costco's mission is "to continually provide our members with quality goods and services at the lowest possible prices." While not every mission will include the word "prices" in it, we know from the hot dog combos and rotisserie chickens that Costco's prices are important in their brand story. And also, even though it uses the word "quality" in it, you can see how this mission aligns with what I define as a "value" business—the focus is on the lowest possible prices, not on the highest quality stuff regardless of the price. When your pricing, brand values, and everything else you've been working on in this book align, it creates this beautiful, virtuous cycle that continually reinforces itself over and over, making buying from you that much easier.

On the other end of the spectrum from Costco, Louis Vuitton's mission states, "Our products are designed to last from generation to generation, aligned with our vision of a truly timeless art de vivre." Talk about carefully chosen words that **prime** for luxury and investment (clearly, a "quality" brand). You know it will be expensive today, but if it is meant to last for generations, it's worth it! (Again, this shows there is great value when you invest in one of their pieces, but it is clearly a quality brand and not a value brand.)

Let's play a game, shall we? This exercise is designed to help you think about the impact of brand identity on perceived value and differentiation. As you go through the exercise, consider how your expectations of the product and its price are influenced by the brand's reputation and image. The following chart includes a list of brands. Imagine they are all coming out with their own branded coffee mug. When you see the name, I want you to write the first word that comes to your mind. Then, list how much you think their coffee mug will cost and what will make it different:

BRAND	FIRST WORD THAT COMES TO MIND	PRICE OF THEIR MUG	WHAT MAKES THEIR MUG UNIQUE
Costco			
Disney			
Louis Vuitton			
Walmart			
Apple			
Netflix			
Tesla			

Even if you have never purchased from a particular listed brand before, you
still have a memory of layered associations that would help you come up with
something. And I'm guessing your prices for each mug aren't the same, right?
And that doesn't mean people won't buy them! What does this teach you about
your company?

TASK: RECONFIRM YOUR BRAND TYPE

Now that you have considered the customer and the market, it is a good time
to pause and reevaluate the company type you selected at the beginning of
Part II. Does it still fit? If not, give yourself permission to change course. After

all, the work you have done to this point is just research and taking notes. The stakes for switching now are much lower than if you ignore that feeling and push forward with a disjointed strategy.

And remember that both strategies can work—neither is wrong as long as you commit to your choice. The most important thing is that you and the rest of the organization really believe in whatever model you choose.

If you are having a hard time, try to step away from what you think you "should" do and what others are telling you is best or what everyone else in your industry is doing. When you stop and think about the options, what do you constantly gravitate toward? Which one gets you and the team energized? Which one makes you stressed out and leaves you feeling like you would hate it? Trust your instincts.

TASK: CONSIDER YOUR MODEL

In addition to knowing your brand type, you also need to know the way people buy from you and how that will line up with your overall pricing strategy. This is the time to decide if your offering will be something people buy as they need the product/service, or as part of a subscription service or membership model. As with determining your brand type, don't feel obligated to mirror what others in your industry are doing.

The "buy when you need it" model, as the name suggests, refers to customers purchasing your product or service only when they need it, so we likely don't need to explain much about that option. But memberships and subscriptions can get a little muddy for people (since they both have payments on a regular basis). So, let's take a moment to explain the main differences between a membership and a subscription:

- Memberships tend to be built on community, while subscriptions can bring value to an individual user without a larger community.
- Memberships can be exclusive, while subscriptions are more likely to want to have a larger customer base to not limit their growth.

Your business has the freedom to choose whatever path you prefer. However, if you're unsure where to start, here's a general rule to guide your decision-making process. In general, value brands are more closely aligned to a subscription model and quality brands are a better fit for memberships.

Let me show you what this can look like in the clothing industry. For a very long time, this was a space where people bought individual items when they needed them. A company's income was dependent upon someone having a need and being motivated enough to finally go to the store to make a purchase (and as the store, you had to hope your advertisements had done enough to make them choose to come to your establishment instead of your competition).

Let's consider an example of a business that decided to try something new. Stitch Fix, a subscription service, is different. They have changed the way people acquire clothes. Items arrive at the customer's house on a regular basis (typically monthly, but most subscription services let the customer pick their preferred frequency), which a "stylist" has chosen for them based on their preferences. The customer tries on the items in the comfort of their own home and sends back anything they don't want. They are only charged for what they keep. Easy. With Stitch Fix, you pay a $20 styling fee per "fix" which gets credited toward your total if you decide to keep anything. If you don't keep anything, the only cost to you is that $20 styling fee. Whether other people buy or not doesn't impact your purchases.

Now, let's look at a membership model. Rent The Runway is a membership-based business where you can borrow items—everything from fancy gowns to sweaters—and send them back when you are done. You can rent one-off items or opt for an ongoing membership where you can have up to five items on loan to you at any given time. The price remains the same each month whether you are renting $1,000 gowns or $40 tops, so it adjusts with your needs (and you don't have to pay a bunch of money for a dress you'll only wear once). This membership model only works if there are other people renting, not buying, and using the items (but not so many that there aren't items available when you want and need them). It also gives its members access to luxury brands they may not have bought otherwise (which is a win for those brands as well).

These examples show how the different models can work in a product–based industry, so let's take a look at services as well. If you offer services, you should start by considering if you work on individual projects and other one-off sales or if you have a retainer model. It is okay to offer both, but know who is a fit for which option and why you would suggest one over the other in a given situation. This should be beyond a "because they asked for it" response. Try to understand what would make someone a fit for each option to determine which model aligns with the type of company you want to be.

These days it is very common for service–based businesses (especially thought leaders, creators, and influencers) to offer memberships through companies like Patreon, Mighty Networks, MemberVault, and others to give their followers additional access or perks for a monthly fee. These could be their main source of income—perhaps their sole source—or be offered on top of those one-off projects and retainers. Whatever the full business strategy you choose, incorporating a membership or subscription can help stabilize income where it might otherwise be unpredictable.

For example, an artist may do commissions and sell pieces off of their website, but that is reliant upon how fast they can make pieces. There isn't a ton of scalability in that, which can limit income. To scale up via membership or subscription offerings, this artist could record their work on video, which can be showcased on social media to gain a following, and then have a Patreon account where they charge $10 (or $5 or $25 or whatever) a month for people to support their content creation and also get prints or tips for doing their own art. This membership / subscription model adds some predictable income and stability between the creation of individual pieces and helps their expertise to impact more people.

Whatever approach you choose is totally fine, and as you can see in that artist example, it is common to have more than one model in place. However, I recommend mastering one approach before venturing into others. Creating multiple customer journeys can lead to confusion, overburden your staff, and dilute your impact.

Just as with your company type, choosing your business model is crucial. Understand why you've chosen it and why other models didn't fit. Be able to articulate why this model benefits your customer.

While you don't have to emulate your competitors, this is a good time to revisit that competition list you created in the last chapter: Make a note of what type of brand each company is (quality or value) and what model they offer (buy when you need it, subscription, membership, mix). If every single one is a value brand, what might a quality brand look like in your industry? If there are tons of buy-when-you-need-it companies in your space, what benefit would customers gain from a membership or subscription? Don't feel like you have to be like everyone else—fight that **herding** instinct! Finding a spot with less competition is awesome because those customers are likely underserved.

TASK: VALUE BRANDS— CONSIDER YOUR DISCOUNT PLAN

Many businesses leverage sales and discounts as key strategies for attracting and retaining customers. This is particularly common among value brands, though not all discount plans are created equal. The biggest mistake I see businesses make when it comes to discounts is using them as a crutch. When unsure about the price, it is common to slap on a discount to make it easier for the team to sell. If you raise your prices by 10 percent and then give your staff a 10 percent discount they can offer whenever they want... did you truly raise the price?

This is why I want you to decide now (while in a **cold state**, away from the pressure of the selling moment) where, when, why, and how your company will discount. Making the decision up front will help you hold yourself and the team to it when you get into a **hot state** and want to lean on a discount to make the pricing and pitching process more comfortable.

Consider the following:

- What is the strategy behind your discounts?
- Why do you need them?
- What format are they? (percentage off, dollars off, coupon, bundling discounts, cash back, buy one get one free)
- What will you not do?
- Why will you not do that type of discount?
- What if you didn't do discounts? (for example, if you choose to have everyday low prices and not do sales)
- How long will they run?
- When will they end?

TASK: CONSIDER A SATISFACTION GUARANTEE

Besides discounts, there's another approach that can greatly enhance customer confidence: satisfaction guarantees. Such guarantees, whether they offer money-back options, store credits, or product returns, provide a preemptive safety net for customers. They help overcome the purchasing hurdle by offering a no-risk trial of the product or service. In general, these types of guarantees make it so more people buy than end up returning what they bought, so they are almost always a good strategy. Do your due diligence to see if they are a fit for you, but also keep in mind that they are likely worth trying and testing to see how they *can* work for you. It may feel scary to add a satisfaction guarantee, but remember, it doesn't have to be forever. One thing I really like about these is that they help ensure a company will challenge themselves to provide services and products that are so great people wouldn't even think to take advantage of the return policy / satisfaction guarantee. This also helps companies to underpromise and overdeliver, which helps customers to be happier, which is valuable all the way around.

Take a moment to consider now: If you were to offer a satisfaction guarantee, what might that look like? How could you make it work? Where can you showcase it to help your potential customers feel good about buying?

As with everything you have learned about so far in this book, however you choose to move forward, whatever your model, business type, and discounting plan (if you have one), it can all work. Clarity on what you are doing and why—and what you will *not* do and why—is the most important thing to keep your brand cohesive and create an easier path to buying for your customer. Remember the example a few pages back about LEGO and your brand memory. You want to be as specific as possible for yourself and your team and every decision the company makes so that the customer can see and align your brand with those same values on a subconscious level.

FROM THIS CHAPTER

Tasks:

- Reconfirm your brand type.
- Consider your model.
- Value brands—consider your discount plan.
- Consider a satisfaction guarantee.

Key Terms:

- Quality Business
- Value Business
- Loss Aversion
- Cognitive Pressure / Cognitive Load
- Prime / Priming
- Herding
- Cold State
- Hot State

CHAPTER 8

THE OFFER

Now that you understand your customer, the market, and your company, let's create the **best offer** for your ideal customer. Even if your business sells hundreds of items, focus on just one as we proceed through this book. Yes, just one. The product or service that you choose in this chapter will become the base of the pricing strategy we create together—what we will call your "best offer." If you have multiple customer personas, products, or services, you can repeat this process for each one. However, focus on one at a time, especially when you're just starting. The steps in this book are meant to be used and applied in every category (and a lot of the work you complete the first time through can translate across multiple products and services, so it will likely get easier and faster with each new pricing plan).

TASK: CONSIDER YOUR OPTIONS

The point of this exercise is to help ensure the offer you focus on (the "best offer" you choose) is aligned with the customer journey and your company type (quality or value). Even if you have something you already believe is the right focus, I still recommend going through this exercise to discover if there are any modifications that could enhance it before you get too far into the pricing process. Let's initiate this process by contemplating three crucial questions:

- What do you want to be known for? (This is about your brand reputation.)
- What is the pain point this product or service is going to alleviate for the customer? (This addresses your value proposition.)

- If people will only get one thing from you, what should it be? (This encapsulates your core offering.)

Don't get hung up on what is currently your most popular item. While acknowledging your existing customer base and learning from past actions is crucial, focus on future aspirations. Your past provides valuable lessons, but it should not restrict your future plans. In the future, what do you want to be doing? What is the dream?

Right now, while you are putting in the effort to construct a behavioral strategy for your pricing, you have the opportunity to build something that will be the foundation of how your business makes money moving forward. In that case, it should be something you are excited about focusing on for a long time. Don't let your own **status quo bias** and **loss aversion** keep you locked into an old strategy that doesn't fit the new dream. What is your business vision for the next five or ten years, and how does your selected product or service align with that vision? It may be something that already exists, you may need to modify an existing offer (perhaps combining some things together or removing aspects that aren't relevant), or you may want to build something completely from scratch. Wherever you land at the end, I recommend you approach this exercise with the mindset that everything is on the table and nothing is set in stone. Not being locked into anything allows you to see everything with fresh eyes.

Start by listing all the products, services, and offerings that could be the best offer. Again, these can be things that already exist, items that are on your roadmap, or brand-new offerings. And, while existing products and services are of course welcome to be on the list, fight the urge to copy over a list from your website or print something from your internal files. This is another point where **loss aversion** and FOMO can trick you into keeping outdated offerings or models. If you are staring at everything that exists, it will limit your thinking.

That is one of the reasons I recommend you do this exercise without technology if possible. Gather all the stakeholders—the people whose input is crucial to the decision-making process—in a room and distribute a stack of Post-it notes to each participant, preferably in various colors (more on the importance of this in a moment). They even make them in different sizes and shapes now, so incorporate variation when you can. You can also mix the types and colors of pens to keep it interesting.

What about remote teams? This exercise can be conducted virtually if you can't gather everyone in a physical location. If you are doing this virtually, set some ground rules so everyone knows they need to turn their cameras on and distractions off. Close email. Close browser windows. Put phones in another room or at least out of sight with notifications off. This is a time for connected, focused work together that needs everyone's commitment to be successful. Use breakout rooms and have a dedicated moderator to keep the conversation moving forward.

Whether you are in person or virtual, when I say to incorporate "everyone important to the conversation," I want you to think beyond the typical boardroom approach. If possible, include representatives from all levels of your organization to incorporate diverse perspectives. While C-level executives provide strategic insight, those on the front lines offer an invaluable perspective on customer interactions and daily operations—both are important for your success. Incorporating representatives from various areas into the conversation early can increase the likelihood they will become advocates (this leverages the **IKEA effect**, which is when people like things they have a part in creating better than those they don't)[52] instead of detractors (intentionally or unintentionally talking around your well-laid plans for something that makes more sense in the real world). And diversity of thought is always valuable when planning. For this reason, you should also get a mix of tenure from the employees who are on the team—newer employees have different insights because they haven't yet fallen into the "that's just the way we do things around here" trap yet. Their insights will be closer to that of your target market if they aren't indoctrinated into all the jargon yet as well.

However, keep in mind the "too many cooks in the kitchen" problem, where having too many people in the discussion can lead to confusion and hinder decision-making. To facilitate a focused discussion, I recommend you gather a group of up to twelve people. If you need more people involved, break it into multiple meetings.

Ideally, this same group will have been involved in the other tasks and processes throughout this book, but if not, let them know the insights from the work that has already been done. Specifically, this meeting is going to focus on your top three to five moments on the customer journey from the **Nudgeability Quadrant**, which you have continued to build on in the **habits** section of the "market" chapter. It is also important to be sure they are on board with the decisions about the type of company you are (**quality** or **value**) and the pricing model(s) you plan to use (time of purchase, membership, subscription, or a mix).

First, give the group an opportunity to consider the journey and modify the top five **micro-moments** if there is something that was missed in the initial work. This doesn't need to take long, but it is good to have buy-in from the group as you kick things off.

Next, take those three to five most critical customer pain points—issues or problems your customers face that your product or service can solve— and lead the group in discussing where and how your company is best equipped to assist the customer. Where do your existing offerings fit in? What modifications may need to be made? When would a new solution be best? Don't get too hung up on what has been done already or the logistics and items that could cause problems in the execution—this meeting is about broadening the horizon to make sure you are looking at the full landscape before zooming in on some areas of focus. That being said, if the number one

nudgeable moment would cost you millions of dollars to pivot to, but you can serve the number two most important nudgeable moment immediately with almost no shifts, discuss if this is the best place for you to start.

If your team exceeds six people, consider a phased approach: Start with smaller groups, and combine their insights to build a more cohesive journey later in the meeting. You can have the groups work on the same important nudgeable moments or assign different ones to each team. (This is one reason I recommend using Post-it notes: they can be placed anywhere and easily moved around.)

The deliverable for this meeting is agreement on your focus area (i.e., which single nudgeable moment from the three to five you started with you want to focus on, as well as a prioritized list of products or services that line up with it). You can also list what would come next in the pipeline (say, if you aren't sure about the feasibility of the top option or if the first item can be completed very quickly), but be sure there is agreement on what the priority is, what the next steps are, and who is completing them before you adjourn the meeting, including clarity on when you will meet next and what will be done by that next meeting.

Note: You may realize that some things you have always offered don't align well with your customers' needs or your new direction. You may also get back to work and cross-reference with a list of existing products and services only to find that you completely forgot about an entire area during the planning meeting. Resist the urge to find a way to cram those things into the new model—that's your **loss aversion** talking. Sometimes an existing offer should be brought back into the mix, yes. But more often, these forgotten areas are opportunities to let go and free up resources. A host of psychological biases can come up if that conversation is needed, including the **sunk-cost fallacy**, so keep in mind such conversations require finesse. (I have a whole book on how to best present change initiatives at work to encourage the likelihood people will be on board with them, so check out *What Your Employee Needs and Can't Tell You* if you would like support with this area.) Even if people resist the idea of removing an existing line at first, it doesn't mean it is wrong or not worth pursuing.

How long does this take? This depends on your business model's complexity and team size. If you have a relatively simple business model and a small team, this could be done in ninety minutes. Depending on the complexity, it could be much longer. I have had this process span over multiple days with a dedicated room for our colorful Post-its. (Always take photos before you leave for the day, just in case.)

Brainy Tip: While you could try to break this process into lots of smaller meetings over a more extended period of weeks or months, I don't recommend this approach. If you don't invest the time to be thoughtful about everything all at once, you will constantly question the decisions and the process can go on forever. It keeps you in a state of **bikeshedding** and **time discounting** that no one wants. This step is fundamental to your focus as a company and how you can motivate the team to keep them on track. Trust me when I tell you it is worth investing whatever time is needed to get it done, working together with all the key players in one motivating experience that can build momentum for the steps to come.

About Those Post-its...Does Color Really Matter?

Short answer: Yes. In the context of behavioral economics and being more brain friendly, every detail (including color), can influence decision-making and engagement. Our predictability-loving subconscious brains make decisions based on associations, which is why **priming**—with images, words, and the whimsy of colorful notes instead of lined paper—matters. Here's a real-life example:

At a 2018 event for 150 executives, McKinsey had the group work in pairs to develop ideas for the coming year's leadership program.[53] Unbeknownst to the participants, the teams were split into two groups, which we will call "cold" and "warm." All had the same task, but there were a few differences in execution.

- Group 1 (Cold)
  - Received firm instructions ("Please adhere to these instructions during the session on ideation" and "You should ensure you are properly hydrated during the session")
  - Were provided ice water to drink
  - Were instructed to write "clearly listed and numbered" responses on white, lined paper

- Group 2 (Warm)
  - Received friendly instructions ("Hello!" "We need your help," and "Thank you")
  - Were provided hot tea or coffee to drink and were encouraged to offer drinks to others
  - Were asked to write their ideas down on sticky notes using colored pencils

So, what happened?

The "cold" group came up with thirty-two ideas, primarily logistical and structural (i.e., don't schedule too many speakers too quickly; make sure breakfast and lunch are on the agenda). The "warm" group generated seventy ideas, which were much more innovative (i.e., host a post-apocalyptic simulation; team building via white water rafting).

McKinsey had several primes running through that test, including the temperature of the beverages, the tone of the instructions, the style of note-taking, and encouraging generosity amongst participants (or not).

While some studies have shown warm beverages to be linked to feeling warmer toward others, this isn't always the right drink choice.[54] However, you can *always* encourage people to be generous and offer a drink to others. This action can promote a spirit of collaboration foundational to teamwork and innovation. And when you want to encourage creativity and thoughtfulness, it's best to ditch the lined paper and strict instructions. This is why I recommend always using Post-its—and colorful ones at that—for an exercise where you want the team to be creative and innovative. This approach gives the brain the freedom to wander and find less common associations in a way that typing into a document or writing on a single sheet of paper just won't. It is a simple investment that can set you up for success in a way that will pay dividends for many years to come.

TASK: CHOOSE YOUR FOCUS

Your big strategic planning meeting is done. You've collected the ideas (and transferred your Post-it notes to a more cohesive document) and have prioritized one nudgeable moment. Now is the moment of truth—the time to pick the most important product or service that will be the best offer for your customer in that nudgeable moment.

- What is the one most important offering you will focus on (your "best offer")?
- Why is this the most important thing?

- What would most likely distract you (i.e., that shiny other project that could be more fun but isn't as important for your customers and what they value)?
- How will you keep yourself from getting distracted?
- Who will hold you accountable?

Resist the urge to just think these through and not write them down. Document this somewhere and keep it close to **prime** yourself and the team for success (and keep you on track when those "shiny objects" come along as your motivation inevitably wanes).

FROM THIS CHAPTER

Tasks:

- Consider your options.
- Choose your focus.

Key Terms:

- Best Offer
- Quality Business
- Value Business
- Loss Aversion
- Status Quo Bias
- IKEA Effect
- Nudge / Nudgeable / Nudgeability Quadrant

- Habits
- Micro-Moments
- Sunk-Cost Fallacy
- Bikeshedding
- Time Discounting
- Priming

CHAPTER 9

THE NUMBERS

As a business owner, things are getting exciting now—you know what your product or service is, who your target audience is, why they value your offering, and how it aligns with your company's mission and vision. In this chapter, we'll dive into the financial aspects of your business. That includes an examination of key numbers like your projected revenue, costs, and net income, in a balance with your personal goals as you build out the future of your business. The structure and order of the questions in this chapter are built to help you overcome the natural tendencies for **planning fallacy** and **optimism bias** to increase your chances for success.

If you already have mountains of numbers and data or you are lucky enough to have a team or department you can reach out to for all the numbers and analyses you want, this is probably a moment you've been eagerly awaiting. That being said, I know that many others reading this book absolutely hate thinking and talking about the numbers. If that is you, the entire idea of this chapter freaks you out (although that is potentially why you bought this book in the first place). And I know that there is a whole other group of readers who would love to have the data and numbers, but lack the time or capacity right now to know much more than some basic points.

No matter which persona resonates with you, there's good news. This chapter will equip you with the insights to make sound decisions about your business financials without delving too deep into complex calculations. Plenty of great books, resources, and courses exist to help anyone understand accounting, ratios, and other number-based analyses to gauge the health of your business. All of that is very important for every company and should be part of your overall corporate strategy. That being said, it is not our focus in this book. This book delves into the psychological aspects of business using strategic questions and insights grounded in neuroscience, highlighting the areas where business people often face hurdles while planning and implementing their pricing strategy. Those brain tricks can make people do strange things, including charging far less than they should or focusing on things that don't move the needle.

So, while this chapter is about the numbers, you won't be setting your final prices just yet—that comes in Part III. This is the pre-work to ensure you set up final pricing that is profitable and sustainable for your business. Throughout this chapter, there are several aspects that apply to every business, but what you look at and the main questions you ask come in two different journeys. While we divided the advice in the book on business type (**quality** or **value**) in this chapter, we are differentiating by what you sell: products or services.

A STRANGE BRAIN FLIP

Time and time again, people come to me feeling completely overwhelmed by everything they feel they need to do to get their message out and sell to the masses. These days, businesses have to be everywhere to reach potential customers (or at least it feels that way). When you decide where to invest your company's time, effort, and budget, there are seemingly endless options. For social media, should you be on LinkedIn, X (Twitter), Threads, Instagram, Facebook, TikTok, Pinterest, YouTube, or whatever other channel will inevitably pop up tomorrow? If you want to establish thought leadership and share longer written content, do you do that in a blog, answer questions on Reddit, create a SubStack, start a podcast, pitch to be on TV, or write articles for established publications? What about attracting and connecting with potential fans? Do you focus on your website, newsletters, advertising, or other channels?

We constantly see stories of people and companies that have gone viral and made millions or billions by leveraging these platforms. But with hundreds of millions of potential customers spread across those platforms...how do you choose?

Bikeshedding Alert! This is where your brain will capitalize on your overwhelm and give you lots of productive procrastination to keep you stuck even though you are so close to the finish line. Your brain is going to want you to jump into the rabbit holes of googling success stories and the "three easy ways to gain a million followers in ten minutes with almost no effort." It's important to resist this temptation.

Here's an intriguing aspect of how our brains function: Even though you've just gone through the process of narrowing down your target customer base, your brain might still push you to reach as many people as possible. The need to be visible and relevant to the greater masses may start nagging at you incessantly. Again, those reading this who are working for large corporations can celebrate that they have teams of people who can help spread the message across many different channels. If this is you, your challenge is to get many people with different bosses and priorities to do what you know is the right approach, even though it is different from what others might be saying or how things have always been done (i.e., the **status quo**). If you struggle with this, check out my other book, *What Your Employees Need and Can't Tell You*, which is all about using brain science to increase your influence in an organization.

For everyone else, you need to narrow your focus and prioritize (are you seeing a theme here?). If you try to do a little bit everywhere, you will never be seen anywhere. This is why we did the work to narrow your audience and understand the customer: so you can determine where it is worth investing your resources to get the best use of your limited time and money to promote your offer. Remember, you are working to build a memory for your potential customers. That means they need to see you consistently in their favorite place. So, wherever that is for you, put your efforts into that one channel so you can build it up. Once it is thriving, you can decide if you want or need to add another.

TASK: WHAT DO YOU REALLY NEED?

We need to flip things back the right way to get your bikeshedding brain to move forward. Right now, your brain is focused on all the opportunities—the millions or billions of potential impressions. Forget that. Take a step back and ask: What does the company really need?

To find the answer, I have a series of questions for you to complete. Getting there is slightly different for service– and product–based businesses, so your questions are listed separately.

SERVICE-BASED BUSINESSES

How much money does your business need to make this year? This is to be financially stable. Be sure to know both the gross number (total of sales before expenses) and the net (what is left for the business and/or your take-home salary after expenses). Whatever you think the number is, add 10 percent to be safe.

How much would ideally come from the offer you are focused on now? Diversifying your income stream is a good idea (just ask anyone whose entire business was through in-person events before the pandemic). Know the gross and net dollar amounts (or whatever your currency of choice) and the percentage of your full business sales that this offer could generate.

Ideally, how many hours would you work per day or week? Even if you love your work and are incredibly passionate about it, you probably want some time off. Are you building a model to sustain that? This is your opportunity to dream into the future. Imagine it is five years from now, and everything is fantastic—how many hours do you work per week? What days do you take off? Vacations? If you want a four-day work week or to be done at three o'clock every day, you need to plan and price to make that happen. If the company has multiple employees (or you plan to add them in the future), consider this for the overall culture of the organization you are building and what your company values are.

How many clients can you realistically work with in a day/week/ month and do your job well? There are a couple of sides to this one. First, people in service-based businesses almost always forget about all the "other stuff" that goes into the work they do for the time they charge for. Regardless of the type of work you do and the specific nature of your client interactions, proper preparation and completing follow-up tasks are both integral to a great engagement. This includes the emails you need to send back and forth, reading any necessary materials before a meeting, time to create a report or recap of the meeting, the time to decompress after the meeting so you can be ready for your next client...the list goes on, and these add up. This is where **planning fallacy** will tank your profitability if you aren't careful. These things always happen; they take up your time and need to be planned for. A one-hour session is never one hour. For some, it is ninety minutes; for others, it could be three or four hours of other work. Whatever "other work" goes into doing the job so your clients rave about it, plan and account for this time.

Second, consider your schedule. Some people prefer to have a couple of days that are back-to-back meetings and other days where they do all the recap, reporting, and preparing for the next day. Over the years, I have learned that this format doesn't work for me, so I schedule buffers around client calls. I typically allot fifteen to thirty minutes before a call to get ready and another thirty minutes after the call to do the recap, send my follow-up email, ensure the next call is on the calendar, and decompress before preparing to give my full attention to the next client. Optimism bias and planning fallacy would say that I could have four or five clients a day, every day, in this model, but that isn't realistic. I would get burned out, and doing it that way doesn't leave room for all the other things that are important to my business model. Because of this, it is essential to set realistic goals and limits for each product type or way my time is spent, including one-off clients, retainers, projects, speaking, and creating content. For clients who want a single one-hour strategy session, there may be five spots per week, but never more than three in a day. (Scheduling software is a great way to stick to this type of model. I use Calendly.)

This is the stage where you may start to worry again. You may be thinking, "What if a potential customer is only available for a meeting on Wednesday and I've already filled my schedule?" or "What if I get busy and there aren't times available for weeks?" The answer is: That is a *good* thing. Remember Supreme and the power of **scarcity**. Time is your most fantastic resource. Having *fewer* options helps the client realize your time is in high demand (**social proof**), so they better grab a time while they can (and come prepared to make the most of it). If this becomes a massive problem and the waitlists are way too long, you can deal with that "problem" when you get there. (What a problem to have, right?!) At that point, you can hire other team members to support you (because you've priced appropriately and are profitable with all those clients) or raise your prices—or both.

To recap, after considering these aspects, you should know how many clients you can realistically work with in a day/week/month to do your job well.

How many clients would you have per year if your schedule was filled to your maximum desired capacity? This is a straightforward calculation based on your monthly or weekly numbers from the past question. Just be sure to include vacations and other important balance points so you (and your team, if applicable) can provide the best service for your clients each day.

Divide the revenue you need to generate next year by the number of clients—how does that compare to what you are currently charging (or were planning to charge, if this is a new venture)? Don't be scared if there is a big gap between the two numbers. That is why we went through this exercise, and you always have options. There is a four-point continuum for you to consider here, concerning: price, number of clients, total revenue, and business type. Where is there wiggle room? If you said that you want to make $500,000 per year and ideally only work with one client per day, and you are charging $100 for the one client meeting—something's gotta give. Do you only need to make $100,000 per year? Could you work with more people? How much more should your hourly rate be? And how does this all tie back to the type of company you said you were?

Remember that it isn't always about you doing more work. If you are working with fewer people, are there enough of them that are willing to pay $2,000 per session to keep your client roster full? Maybe you have two clients per day, and they are paying $1,000 each. Revisit the lessons in the "you" chapter if you need some inspiration. While you are not limited to what the market is charging, it is good to revisit the numbers you got from your competitive analysis to see where you might fall in the mix as you plan. And take a moment to reflect on the type of business you selected in the "company" chapter. If you said you are a "value" business and have chosen a price point that is triple that of your competition, one of those things will need to change.

Once you finish this step, you should have a general number of where you want and need to be for your pricing. You don't need to know the final number yet, but write down some of the boundaries of where you want to be.

How many new clients are you looking to add per month (or over the year) to hit your numbers? What I find time and time again in this process is when I ask a client what the "dream" would be for how many new clients they would sign in the next year, it is usually achievable. Ten. Fifty. A hundred. What is your number?

Whatever it is, it is probably pretty reasonable. (Note: if you have a team of people doing these services within your company, you need to go through these steps for each person and then divide the total number of clients needed by the number of staff you have—or will have—to deliver the level of service you are promising.) And again, whatever that number is, I am guessing it is far less than where you started in feeling overwhelmed and needing to get millions of impressions on all the social media channels.

If you want to sign one new client a month, or two a week, that is super reasonable (and is much more likely to happen with a focused approach). You probably already know ten people who would be great fits for the work you do! Focus on being seen by *them*, and don't worry about the masses. That focused approach will help you spend less time and money on bikeshedding and free you up to focus on the stuff that matters (like updating your pricing page on your website, creating a great lead magnet and drip campaign, having a solid presence on your chosen channel, and making consistent outbound sales calls).

And yes, you know I will give you the tools to do just that. For now, focus on feeling good about those numbers.

PRODUCT-BASED BUSINESSES

How much money does your business need to make this year? This is to be financially stable. Be sure to determine both the gross number (the full dollar amount of sales before expenses) and the net (what is left for the business and/or your take-home salary after expenses). Remember to include both fixed and variable expenses and factor in paying yourself, as well as money to invest in marketing and advertising. Whatever you think the number is, add 10 percent to be safe.

How much would ideally come from the offer you are focused on now? Diversifying your income stream is a good idea; most product-based businesses sell more than one thing. Since you're focusing on one product at a time in this process, it's important to understand what portion of your overall business goals this product represents. That can help you get clear on how much time, advertising, and other resources to devote to promoting this item. Know the gross and net both in dollar amounts (or these amounts in your currency of choice) and as percentages of your full business sales.

Ideally, how many hours would you work per day or week? This question is important for everyone—especially for the "makers" out there. Even if you love the pieces you are creating and are incredibly passionate about them, you probably want some time off. Are you building a model to sustain that? This is your opportunity to visualize your future business model and working conditions. Imagine it is five years from now and everything is amazing—how many hours do you work per week? What days do you take off? Vacations? If you want a four-day work week, to be done at three o'clock every day, or to eventually turn your side hustle into your full-time job, you need to plan and price to make that happen. If the company has multiple employees (or you plan to add them in the future), consider this for the overall culture of the organization you are building and what your company values are.

What is the realistic quantity of products you can create or package daily, weekly, or monthly without compromising your well-being?
Again, this question is especially important for those in manufacturing or creative industries to avoid burnout. Sure, you could work eighteen or twenty hours a day, only taking a break when your vision gets blurry or your hands cramp up, but that isn't sustainable. As companies grow, these items can be outsourced so you create and send pieces even while sleeping. But that is only possible if you plan and price properly.

When you look at your capacity and schedule, for whatever level your business is at now, what is the maximum reasonable daily/weekly/monthly capacity that allows you to maintain the quality you promise to your clients? (Of course, this is different based on the type of business you selected in the "company" chapter—if you are a "value" brand, your answer will be very different from the "quality" brand.) This may be limited (or stretched) by the capacity of a factory you are using to produce items, the availability of raw materials, or the human capacity of how long it takes to create a piece—or (more likely) some combination of those items.

And be sure to balance this with the capacity across all your product lines based on the percentage of your revenue you identified needing to come from this item.

Whatever your number, avoid the **planning fallacy** and **optimism bias** trap that is going to make you want to say, "Well, I know we typically make eight of these in an hour, so let's round it up to ten because I'm sure we will gain efficiency over time." Be realistic and price for what *is*, not what might happen someday. If you get more efficient as time goes on, your profits will go up, which is terrific, but don't price today for an optimized system that *might* exist a year from now. If you can only make eight in an hour and can only reasonably do that for six hours in a day, be honest about it. This is your business, after all. Who are you trying to trick with these little stretches and idealisms? (Remember: It's not you, it's your brain. So, this is your opportunity to outsmart it and resist those temptations.)

Brainy Tip: Speaking of planning fallacy and optimism bias, don't build the plan so you only make enough if you work to the max every single day or if every single item sells out. You will get sick. Something will happen with your supply chain. Things will go wrong. Price so you have some wiggle room in your margins.

How many units can you sell per year? This can be calculated based on your monthly or weekly production rates that we discussed earlier. However, you need to be sure to work in vacations and other essential points of balance, as well as the seasonality of the product if that is a concern. Most products are not in the same demand all year with no fluctuation. What are your busy times, and when are there lulls? You can produce year-round to keep stocking up for busy times (being sure to factor in the storage costs), but when you consider the total units sold, keep this in mind. If you have any historic numbers from this or other products (or from the competition), this data is useful to look at now.

Divide the number you need to make next year by the number of units you can sell—how does that compare to what you are currently charging (or are planning to charge, if this is a new venture)? Don't be scared if there is a big gap between the two numbers. That is why we went through this exercise, and you always have options. Now is when you negotiate a bit on the key aspects of your business—what I call your five-point continuum. These five points are price, number of units, quality, revenue, and business type. Where is there wiggle room? If you said that you want to make $500,000 per year, and you can only make four items per day and you are charging $20 for each item...something's gotta give. Do you only need to make $100,000 per year? How can you increase production? How much more should people pay for this?

Remember, it isn't always about you doing more work. If your product is **scarce**, that can increase willingness to pay. Limited quantities and custom pieces can be a great thing for pricing—but you need to be sure this scarcity aligns with the type of business you are. (If you chose "value" as your business type and realized here you need to charge three times what your competitors are asking, that will be a problem.)

While you are not limited to what the market is charging, it is good to revisit the numbers you got from your competitive analysis, along with your company type, so you see where you might fall in the mix as you plan and ensure it will all make sense for the customer.

Once you finish this step, you should have a general number of where you want and need to be for your pricing. You don't need to know the final number yet, but write down some of the boundaries of where you want to be.

How many monthly (or annual) sales do you need to hit your goals?
Again, remember your seasonality factors here. Whatever that number, I'm guessing it's less than the millions or billions of impressions you thought you needed that were weighing you down and keeping you stuck. For a custom-made

art brand, this could be twenty-four clients in a year—just two per month—to hit the revenue goals.

Be sure the number is reasonable for where you are. It is easy to get swept up in the success stories on social media that show how someone is making hundreds of thousands of dollars per month or went from zero to 300,000 units in six months, but keep in mind that these stories are not the norm. I deeply hope you end up being one of those amazing success stories, but don't build a business that will only work if you are.

Brainy Tip: If you are looking for more insights on creating businesses that scale, I highly recommend reading *The Voltage Effect* by John List, and checking out our conversation from when he was on *The Brainy Business*.[55]

DON'T MISS WHAT'S MISSING

We humans are prone to **survivorship bias**, which happens when we are missing what's missing.[56] This tendency got its name during World War II, when the Allies were looking for ways to ensure more of their planes (and pilots) got home safely. They couldn't reinforce every area of the planes with super-strong metals (there is a reason tanks can't fly), so they did an analysis showing where all the bullet holes were on the planes. They plotted them all together to find the trends and determine where to place the metal. The response was something along the lines of, "Great! If that is where the bullet holes are, that is what we will reinforce. Thanks!"

Do you see the flaw in the logic?

Thankfully, the researchers did and pointed out that a massive (and critical) data set was missing. What about all the planes and pilots that didn't make it back to be part of the analysis? They were likely shot in the places where the surviving planes *didn't have* bullet holes. (You know, the engine, the cockpit…things like that.) Those were the actual places to reinforce. Can you imagine how history might have been different if they didn't remember to include the missing data set?

Be wary of any content you see about people who have made millions by doing "this one thing" or "that amazingly simple trick" that *all* successful business owners do. Those stories are missing what's missing. For example, if it says that "all" successful business owners get up at four in the morning, how did they reach that conclusion? They potentially asked people who *did* get up early and *were* successful business owners, but what about all the people who get up at four in the morning and are not successful? What about all the successful business owners that get up later? There is a lot of data missing in those stories. Hopefully, now that you know about survivorship bias, you won't get swept up in the extremes of over-optimism or pessimism and can set a more realistic price.

Hate The Idea of Raising Prices? Try This Mental Trick

If you're struggling with the idea of raising prices, I've got a simple, game-changing tip.

Imagine you sell water bottles. Yours currently sells for $8, and you need to raise the price to $12. This is a substantial increase, which may feel mentally jarring and lead you to offer discounts before people ask for them or completely put off the process of raising the price.

Step back and ask: "What if tomorrow we sold this for ten times what we charge now?" This creates a new, high mental **anchor** of $80. How could you justify this price or add value to the item? A limited-edition design or a celebrity using it (**social proof**)? What else? Once you can get behind selling it at $80, selling it for $12 is a breeze.[57]

TASK: LOOK FORWARD AND BACKWARD

Before we close out this chapter and the foundations you've built across Part II, I want you to do two things:

1. Consider what you want your business to look like five years from now. If everything is flourishing and you are living the dream—what is that like? How many customers or clients do you have? Where are you selling? What are your days like? Do you have a team, are you a solo operation, or are you using contractors? How much free time do you have, and what are you using it to do?

   Now, look at the model you have set up in this chapter. Are these plans leading you to where you want to be five or ten years from now? If not, what needs to change?

2. Once that is done, reflect on everything you have done up to this point. Now that you have looked at the numbers you plan to charge, does your pricing align with the customer you are targeting and what they value? Or with how you plan to brand your company? If anything is off, take the time to revisit whatever areas need to be tweaked to fit your goals. It could be any (or all) of the sections. Ideally, you have learned some things along the way that can inform some of the decisions you made earlier in the process. Take some time now to see where adjustments should be made so you feel really good about how everything is aligned before you proceed.

It's understandable if you feel fatigued at this point, but don't give up. It's worthwhile to take a short break, rejuvenate, and discuss your plans with significant others before proceeding. I know you may want to skip this recap and reflection step, but there is a really important reason I include it for you now.

There is a concept in the software industry that if you identify and fix a problem in the planning phases, it is a $10 problem. When you have started building and coding everything, identifying and fixing that same problem could cost $10,000. Once everything is live and you have users, that could easily be a $10 million problem. The lesson for every business is that taking the time up front to be thoughtful and identify those $10 problems before they become much bigger is worth the investment. Of course, you won't catch everything, and you will continue to find and fix problems as they crop up. But since at this point all you have done is plan, anything you fix or adjust is worth investing the time in now before moving forward with Phase III.

Being thoughtful about these pieces will set your brainy business apart from the competition. This is how you win and make sure your pricing is perfectly aligned with your brand so it is easy for people to buy from you. Trust me. It's worth it, and so are you.

FROM THIS CHAPTER

Tasks:

- What do you really need?
- Look forward and backward.

Key Terms:

- Quality Business
- Value Business
- Bikeshedding
- Status Quo Bias
- Planning Fallacy
- Scarcity
- Social Proof
- Optimism Bias
- Survivorship Bias
- Anchoring

PART III
APPLYING
IT

CHAPTER 10

THE FRAMEWORK

Imagine you're strolling down a cobblestone street in the heart of a bustling city with your best friend, Jane. You haven't seen each other in six months, and you are quickly absorbed in a riveting conversation about your latest adventures. Suddenly, a tantalizing aroma drifts its way toward you: the rich scent of melting chocolate, the sweet tang of brown sugar, the creamy fragrance of butter, and a hint of sea salt. It's the unmistakable scent of freshly baked chocolate chip cookies!

You're now on the hunt to find the source of the delightful smell; while you're still both half listening to each other, you've become distracted. You're essentially cartoon characters now, with your noses leading you down the street.

When you finally find the store and see a line out the door, you think, "These cookies must be amazing!" and can't help but wander inside. You're handed a sample and told there is a sale: Today only—buy three, get one free. Before you know it, you and your friend leave the bakery, each eating a cookie, with a bag in hand and an undisclosed number of tasty treats for later.

LET'S TRY THAT AGAIN

Before we break down that experience, I want you to rewind and try it one more time. You and your friend Jane are walking down the same street again, having the same engaging conversation, when, out of nowhere, someone shoves a flyer in your face and says, "Today only! Buy four cookies and only pay for three of them!" And while fumbling with words and maneuvering a tray into your face, he shouts, "I've got samples!"

Ugh.

How rude is this guy? You and your friend, annoyed, decline the samples and can't get away from him fast enough. Instead of continuing your engaging conversation, you've started a one-upping contest of worst sales experiences. By the time you're in front of the bakery, you're so irritated that you grab your phones to write a Yelp review about how awful their tactics are, vowing that you will never buy from them (pitying those fools in line whose standards are lower than your own). The scent barely registers as you continue down the street.

Same bakery. Same cookies. Yet the two experiences stand worlds apart. One pulls you in with an irresistible allure, the other pushes you away with an uncomfortable confrontation. It's a clear demonstration of how experience frames our perceptions.

In the first scenario, you were almost definitely buying. In the second, you were almost definitely *not*. And if you noticed, the price was never a factor. They could have been $3 each in the first scenario and 50 cents apiece in the second. It didn't matter, because again, it's not about the price. And it's not about the *cookie*, either.

Of course, some minimum and maximum assumptions are being made here. If the cookies were $100 each or the samples were stale, it would have impacted the purchase. (Again, these insights I'm giving you aren't magic.) That said, it doesn't mean you would never have bought any cookies. I intentionally said it "would have impacted the purchase" instead of saying, "You would not have bought them." That's not a foregone conclusion (remember our grilled cheese sandwich examples from the beginning of the book).

Now that you have built a foundation around the psychology of yourself, your customer, your company, the market, your offer, and the numbers...it is time to apply it. The first step is to incorporate the fundamental concepts of the "It's Not About the Cookie" framework, which I will break down for you in this chapter.

Six main concepts make up the framework—priming, herding/social proof, loss aversion/perceived ownership, reciprocity, framing, and scarcity—all of which you have been introduced to already throughout the book. In this chapter, I will show you how they fit into the cookie scenarios above and how to prioritize and apply them differently based on which type of business you are. (Note: Your company type is a huge factor in how you work through the framework, so if you haven't finalized it yet or are debating after working through the steps in Part II, take a moment now to finalize and choose whether you are a brand of **value** or **quality**.) Later, in Chapter 13, there are four case studies where I break down how real businesses incorporate these concepts into their strategy, included to help this be even more readily applicable and easy for you. There is one quality product-based business, one quality service-based business, one value product-based business, and one value service-based business so everyone can find at least one case study that relates to their company. Sound good?

Great! Let's kick things off by discussing the six categories of concepts in the "It's Not About the Cookie" framework:

- Priming (the scent of the cookies)
- Herding / Social Proof (the line, reviews)
- Loss Aversion / Perceived Ownership (from the tasting, scent, and scarcity)
- Reciprocity (free sample)

- Framing ("Buy three, get one free" vs. "Buy four cookies and only pay for three of them")

- Scarcity (Today only!)

PRIMING (THE SCENT OF THE COOKIES)

You may have noticed that the same basic things happened in both scenarios—all six concepts from the framework are present in each of them. So, why was the experience so different? The first reason is priming.

If you remember, priming is the concept that whatever happens just before a moment of decision can impact the choice. So, starting with a great "scent" (and removing any not-so-great ones) is imperative to selling at the price point you want.

The right prime will draw people in, and the wrong one will push them away. And as you saw in the two cookie scenarios, having the right prime (in this case, the scent of the cookies) came *first* when you bought the cookies. In the bad scenario that didn't result in a purchase, it came last. This is very important.

Whether you are a value or quality business type, you have to start with priming.

Why does it matter? The scent of the cookies got your subconscious "buying" brain excited and made you interested in getting something sweet. By the time you found the sign for the bakery, you were practically begging them to sell you a cookie—and then they gave you a sample... and a discount! How nice of them! And it is such a great deal, and it is today only...and your conscious brain is going to quickly logic its way into submitting to the will of your subconscious (which is filtering through those eleven million bits of information per second to show you things that support its desire for those delicious cookies).

Begging and shoving logic in the buyer's face does not work—remember the cookie flyer. You got irritated and shunned the whole establishment in that scenario. This is also why you can't jump right in with the pricing. If you start with the price and then plan to follow it up with a bunch of reasons why it is a good investment (or why they'll like it or how valuable it is), they will have already tuned out and moved on.

And no, the service-based businesses and online retailers can't ignore this step. While I've been relating it to the "scent," priming is about much more than this one sense, and it always matters. Powerful imagery, great verbiage, video, emojis—they can all prime your potential customers to take an action (or drive them away).

All the work you have been doing to this point in the book will make it easier to build your primes. And, as you may have guessed, it all comes down to which type of business you are: quality or value.

This is about consistency of messaging. If you are a **quality brand**, how is that seen, heard, felt, smelled, and experienced in every interaction someone has with your brand? High-end shopping experiences often come with perks: Trying on engagement rings? When you sit with the associates at Cartier, expect a glass of their exclusive Cartier Champagne. Or perhaps you would prefer Tiffany & Co., where "they sit you down in cushy velvety chairs, bring you glasses of champagne, and feed you super cutesy Tiffany blue box mini cakes."[58] Now that you're engaged and trying on wedding dresses, if you stop by Vera Wang, you can expect (in addition to the complimentary champagne and cookies) tea served in china from Vera's collection. These are of course in addition to the exquisite finishes, beautiful lighting, custom scents, plush furnishings, and everything else you take in from your first interaction with the brand. Everything exudes quality. Potential customers sense it without you having to say a word because it is so well thought out and cohesive.

What about the value brands? Consider shopping at Costco, for example. Instead of plush carpets and quiet elegance, you walk on polished concrete floors and hear the buzzing of forklifts. It's a warehouse stacked high with bulk goods, where every corner reminds you of how much you're saving. They don't have fancy signage or invest in designing beautiful tags to put on the shelves because that would mean they'd have to increase their prices. WinCo takes this further by having shoppers bag their own groceries. You have been primed to see the value they provide (note that this doesn't mean everything is the lowest price you can possibly find), and the experience is constantly reinforcing that. You know you are getting a great value without them having to say it over and over again.

Whether a brand is one of quality or value, that consistency of messaging needs to be reinforced at every point of interaction. From the chic, minimalist aesthetic of a quality brand's Instagram account to the daily deals posted on a value brand's Twitter, each interaction speaks to the brand's core values. Both types of companies should have a clean website experience, but they are simple in very different ways. Quality brands are showcasing simple elegance. You have a streamlined, beautiful experience because they've carefully curated each element, from the sophisticated font choices to high-quality photography, and even the meticulously chosen names of their categories and headlines whisper luxury. A quick look at the Cartier website and you see the words "timeless" and "iconic." They feature complimentary delivery, easy return or exchange, and free gift wrapping on the home page. Costco's website is simple in a more efficient way. It isn't clunky or cheap, but it is clear they didn't invest in making it ornate and over-the-top. It is clean and organized with headers that include "Deals," "New Lower Prices," "While Supplies Last," and "Get Email Offers." Again, everything is priming for the structure of their company and what they want everyone to know about their brand.

For your business, know that being a quality brand doesn't mean you need your own brand of champagne or to invest massive amounts of money into your website or store fixtures or anything else. Similarly, being a value brand doesn't mean you need to remove everything that may be deemed unnecessary. All of these primes can be implemented across a spectrum, and you need to evaluate what is the best fit for your brand.

TASK: CHOOSE YOUR PRIMING WORDS AND IMAGE INSPIRATION

In my experience, consistently using certain keywords that encapsulate your company's essence significantly improves how people perceive your business. These words should be present in your internal communication, advertisements, sales language, and website—and they should have corresponding imagery to match. Your company type serves as a touchstone to ensure your decisions about time, money, and energy investments align. Similarly, these priming words can guide your communication strategy.

There are three lists below: one with words that are typically associated with quality, one for words that are typically associated with value, and one for words that apply to both. Review the applicable lists and circle (or make note of) any words that resonate with your **best offer**. It is likely there will be lots of crossover with the company itself, but that isn't always the case, which is why this is done separately as you consider the specific placement you are working on. If there are general company priming words that don't apply for this offer, make note of those as well for your

record. Because the intention is for you to do this again and again, there is
a list available for you, along with the other companion documents to this
book, at *thebrainybusiness.com/pricing-book*.

Circle all the words you think relate to the offer you are focusing on.

TYPICAL QUALITY BRAND WORDS				
certified	educated	hard-to-find	precious	sophisticated
couture	eloquent	innovative	premium	stylish
cultured	exclusive	luxury	private	superb
detailed	flawless	perfect	rare	supreme
			state of the art	upscale

TYPICAL VALUE BRAND WORDS				
abundant	efficient	grounded	necessary	reliable
accessible	familiar	known	nimble	scalable
available	fast	lean	obtainable	steady
			quick	ubiquitous

INTERCHANGEABLE WORDS

accurate, adaptable, adventure, ambitious, authentic, balanced, believe, bright, calm, candid, capable, clear, collaboration, commitment, compliant, consistent, cooperative, coordinated, courageous, creativity, credible, curious, decisive, dedicated, deep, delightful, descriptive, different, diligent, discipline, distinct, dramatic, driven, durable, dynamic, empower, energetic, enrich, entertaining, enthusiasm, expanding, famous, fearless, festive, fierce, focused, freedom, frequent, fresh, friendly, fulfillment, futuristic, gratitude, growth, happiness, harmonious, helpful, holistic, honest, important, inquisitive, inspire, instinctive, integrity, intelligent, interesting, involved, knowledgeable, leadership, logical, long-lasting, long-term, love, loyalty, magical, momentous, mysterious, natural, new, next, offbeat, open, optimal, organic, outstanding, passionate, peaceful, perpetual, perseverance, physical, planning, popular, possible, powerful, private, productive, profit, progress, protective, proud, quiet, ready, real, real-time, rebel, receptive, relaxed, relevant, remarkable, resilient, reusable, ripe, robust, safety, sassy, satisfaction, scalable, secure, selective, serious, service-oriented, sharing, sharp, simple, sincere, small, smart, smooth, snarky, solid, special, spectacular, speedy, stable, steadfast, strategic, strong, sturdy, substantial, subtle, successful, succinct, sudden, suitable, sustainable, swanky, tangible, tasteful, teamwork, tested, thankful, thoughtful, timely, traceable, transform, transparent, truthful, uncovered, unique, unknown, upbeat, usable, useful, vast, wacky, weird, well-made, wise, workable, youthful, zesty

Review what you have circled and select your top ten. If there are any words you like that weren't on the list, feel free to use those. This is just a sample of the many available priming words.

Now, take your top ten words and search each of them online. Words have lots of different meanings and associations. Just because you read a word with a particular intention doesn't mean it will mean that (and only that) to a potential audience. It is always a good idea to do some digging and find out what associations might already exist with the words you are thinking of tying to your offer. Don't forget to try the word as a hashtag on various social media sites. What articles and images come up? Are they things you want to have associated with your business? If not, look for related words (a thesaurus is your new best friend), and keep digging until you find words and associated images you like.

After researching all ten words, select your top three. For each, choose a main image from your search results that best represents the feeling you hope to evoke with that word. You can also write an explanation of the thought behind that particular word choice and how it relates to the customer experience and the offer itself.

Brainy Tip: There are lots of fantastic photo sites you can type your words into, so you aren't limited to Google. At the time of this writing, my go-to sites are Adobe, Canva, iStockPhoto, Pexels, and Unsplash.

Incorporate the three chosen words in all related communications such as website descriptions, advertisements, sales scripts, and internal communications. **You don't need all three on everything every time, but you must always have at least one.** When you start to worry that it is too repetitive, remember that potential customers will not see these as often as you do, and consistency is key when forming that memory.

Consider a brand like Apple. Their sleek, minimalist design is instantly recognizable to millions around the world. Even something like their white cords and headphones, which were novel when introduced, are a nod to their "different" approach. You may not consciously realize it, but this reinforces their values in your brain each time you see those items.

Your priming words and images can and should be incorporated into everything your business does. And no item is too ordinary or too small. In reality, those commoditized items are a great opportunity to stand out. For example, I once had a client with very soft business cards—so soft that everyone commented on them. When people would ask about them, her response was something along the lines of, "Thanks! I picked them out myself." I encouraged her to consider how this texture and the moment of connection it creates ties in with her brand promise. She is a consultant, so now she says something along the lines of, "Thanks! It's a reminder of how smooth and easy it is to do business with us." Because they are touching the business card while you say that, it is more likely they will remember you and this conversation and relate that positive trait to your company—win!

Consider all the senses when incorporating priming, and put more thoughtfulness into every moment. Not everything you consider will be incorporated into the final experience, but choosing the right ones can have a considerable impact. And remember how in the bad cookie scenario the scent of the cookies came too late. So, because this is the scent that draws you in, I want you to think about that irresistible *early* moment that will entice people and help their subconscious feel excited about working with you.

This can include a variety of things. It could be your lead magnet or the advertisements you put out. It could even be the colors or styles you and your team wear at events. Your social media presence also plays a part. All these aspects should focus on reinforcing your brand's priming words and associated memories.

HERDING AND SOCIAL PROOF

Because humans are a herding species, once you've piqued their interest with a prime, showing that other people have chosen you is important. In the cookie example, this was the line at the bakery. Your outraged Yelp review showed this section's negative side and why paying attention to your experience is so important.

There are seven main categories of social proof:[59]

- **Customers:** People who buy from you are great resources for others who are considering making a purchase. As a herding species, we look to others like ourselves to help us decide when we aren't sure of the best next step. So, existing customers are really helpful here.

- **Experts:** While your own internal expertise is still important, when looking at social proof, this is more about what external experts say about you. Getting seals of approval from trusted third parties with expertise creates a **halo effect** that helps people feel comfortable about buying from you.

- **Celebrities/Influencers:** You've likely seen this play out again and again. When a celebrity or influencer uses and/or endorses something, those who want to be like them are eager to jump on board. Your influencer/celebrity might also be an expert or a customer, which can be even better. While organic mentions are ideal (so you know they actually love and use/wear that product/brand), this is very commonly something companies pay for and still get value from.

- **Masses (the Wisdom of the Crowd):** Imagine you are going to buy a widget on Amazon. Two nearly identical widgets are for sale. Company A has four reviews/ratings and an average of 4.8 stars. Company B has four *thousand* ratings/reviews and the same average star rating of 4.8. Which one do you choose? What if Company B was more expensive? What if Company B had a star rating of 4.7? 4.6? Chances are, even if Company B is a little more expensive and has a slightly lower star rating, you will feel more comfortable buying from them because there are so many more positive reviews compared to Company A. Only having four reviews feels like a gamble, even with the same rating. This is the power of the masses. This also shows up when you see a brand everywhere (like iPhone, Nike, Coca-Cola, and Starbucks). All those (seemingly happy) customers mean they must be doing something right and are worth the risk to try.

- **Friends/Personal Connections (the Wisdom of Your Friends):** Studies have shown that 83 percent of Americans were more likely to buy a product or service when they received a verbal recommendation from a friend or family member.[60] This is why referral programs exist, and why it is worth investing in stellar experiences people can't help but share about.

- **Certifications:** Much like the experts section, when you have trusted, third-party organizations, associations, or other entities endorse you and your company and/or product or service, it goes a long way to building trust. This often comes with an actual seal of approval in the form of a special logo or recognizable icon.

- **Earned Media:** Not every list you will find on the various types of social proof includes this one, but in the age of pay-to-play campaigns, when a company, person, product, or service is featured in the press and they didn't pay for it, that often holds more weight than when they bought their spot. You can't always tell, but even the perception of earned media can go a long way for your business. This is why companies invest in PR.

TASK: CHOOSE UP TO THREE SOCIAL PROOF TACTICS

All categories of social proof can enhance the credibility of your business, but some may be more effective depending on your specific situation. That being said, if you try to do everything all at once, you won't get anything done (**bikeshedding** alert!), so I've prioritized the seven types of social proof based on your business type. This can help you narrow down your options and focus on the areas that will bring the most bang for your buck.

FOR VALUE BUSINESSES

While not every value-focused business is looking to sell large quantities, it is fairly common because you often make up for your lower margins with volume. For that reason, I put the **masses (wisdom of the crowd)** at the top of your social proof list. You want to show that lots of people love and trust you to make it easy for a prospective customer to feel comfortable buying from you. When this happens, it also lessens the burden on you to rely on a highly trained sales staff because people buy more naturally without that support. That allows you to reduce expenses even more and provide more value. So, invest in getting lots of ratings and reviews and being seen wherever possible.

A very close second to the masses is **customers**, because…you need them to write all those reviews, leave ratings, and be visible using your products and services. While you can incentivize people to leave these ratings and reviews with money, chances to win prizes, free stuff, or access to sales, you don't have to. You will be amazed at how many people are willing to rate and leave reviews if you simply ask. If you don't receive enough reviews or ratings this way, then consider offering an incentive. However, be aware that once you start this, it's difficult to stop. That's why I recommend trying to get reviews organically before resorting to incentives.

Next is your **friends and personal connections**, for the same reason as customers above. You know that 83 percent of people are more likely to buy when they get referrals from friends and family members, so when you ask them to leave a rating, you can also ask them to recommend you to someone they care about. I recommend you combine some specificity in here to make it feel more real and tangible. Instead of saying: "Please refer us," or "We love referrals," or "How likely are you to recommend us?" which aren't very action-oriented, try something like, "Can you think of one friend who would love this too? Please consider sharing it with them." Or "Which two colleagues would be most likely to get value from this? Will you tell them about it?" This **framing** helps it to feel more tangible and easier to take an action on the suggestion. I've seen some really great campaigns where a company will give a sample size item with a customer order and encourage them to share it with a friend or family member who would love it. This is a great way to introduce your product to someone while taking advantage of social proof (and leveraging **reciprocity**, which we will cover later in the chapter).

Earned Media: This is a great option for a value business, because other than the time it takes to pitch and do the interviews, earned media is free! That means you can get great social proof in a way that also keeps costs down. You've probably heard there is "no such thing as bad press." When you are a value business, how cheap you are may become a joke (look at Spirit Airlines, a common focus for late-night hosts to poke fun at in their monologues). Here's the thing; for everyone who is looking for a budget airline, there is no question who is "cheap," and because all airlines have to be safe to meet strict regulations, this press actually aligns with their value proposition. It may feel difficult to have people making fun of you and your company, but try to reframe that in your mind (if it aligns with your mission) and see if this is a positive worth embracing.

Celebrities/influencers, experts, and certifications are all helpful as well, of course. But I recommend you master these other areas first before dabbling in this space.

FOR QUALITY BUSINESSES

There are a couple of different approaches to the quality business type, and which one you are in makes a difference in which areas of social proof I recommend you focus on.

- If your quality is based on knowledge, expertise, sustainability, high levels of corporate social responsibility, a heavy investment in research and development, and/or innovation, I recommend you start with **experts** and **certifications** as your top areas for social proof focus. People need to know you practice what you preach (and that it isn't just *you* saying it, but that it is proven and recognized by others as well).

- If you are a luxury brand, I recommend you focus on **celebrities and influencers**. You need people who can afford your products and who have followings of people who want to emulate what they are wearing, using, eating, driving, etc. If the right people are spotted with your product or known to use your service, their masses will follow (and some of them can afford to buy from you). Investing in expensive ad placements can also be very important here to show that you are successful enough (i.e., enough people are buying from you) to afford them. Those ads can include celebrities and influencers for additional social proof. (Just think of all the red carpets out there where photographers are shouting, "Who are you wearing!?" Many of those items are donated or on loan because of the great press (i.e., social proof) they create for the brand. So, this is an opportunity to get creative.) And don't assume this won't work for you if you can't afford a major celebrity. There are four levels of influencer: Nano-influencers have 1,000 to 10,000 followers, micro-influencers have 10,000 to 100,000 followers, macro-influencers have 100,000 to 1,000,000 followers, and celebrity/mega influencers have over a million followers.[61] There is an influencer to fit every brand size, and they all have their own dedicated followings that can be worth tapping into.

All types of quality brands should also focus on the **friends and personal connections** because word of mouth is key for quality items. You are likely asking people to make a bigger investment than they are making now and/or than what your competition is asking for. So, having referrals and a stamp of approval from a trusted friend or family member will make it easier for them to buy. Quality brands are closely tied to your customers' identity—who they are and who they want to be.[62] When the right group of their peers are recommending a brand, they will be more likely to listen and want to be part of that in-crowd. Every company should also try to get **earned media** whenever possible to help gain status from unbiased third parties.

While some quality brands will benefit from customer testimonials, many are in categories where things like star ratings and reviews from customers are less of a factor in the buying decision. As an example, you will not see star ratings or customer reviews on the Maserati website. If you can afford to buy one and choose to get it, you're going to love it, so reviews like that are out of place. Similarly, you are less likely to care about the masses, because, as a quality brand, you aren't for everyone. If you get lots of buzz from those masses through your earned media or guerilla marketing tactics or celebrity endorsements, that is a bonus, but it shouldn't be your focus.

TASK: GET THEM TALKING

Whether you are trying to create buzz or want influencers or the masses to be creating that social proof for you, you may be wondering...how do you get them talking? Enter the **peak-end rule** and **surprise and delight**.

THE PEAK-END RULE

Your first step is to look at your experience. What is it like to work with you? Where are things great, and where do they get clunky? Are there any really negative points you need to remove from the experience? All company types need to work on and continually optimize their experience. And while there are some times where increasing friction can be helpful for a specific goal, because the vast majority of businesses are too difficult to work with, we are going to focus on reducing friction.

Roger Dooley has written a fantastic book, aptly named *Friction*, which I highly recommend if you are looking for a resource to dig in deeper on how to do this with great examples of what it can look like in real businesses.[63] For our purposes here, your experience is key to the perception people have of your company (think back to the priming section). As you saw there, whether you are a quality brand or one of value, people still appreciate and reward easier experiences. This includes the headline on your ads, the images viewers encounter, the website headers, the text they read there, and even the buttons they click. It also encompasses the forms you ask them to fill in, the interactions they have with your company over the phone, the emails they receive, and how people talk about you on social media, plus every other touchpoint in between.

Paying attention to your experience can feel daunting—if everything matters and there are so many points to consider, how do you know you are choosing the right one? This can become an extreme **bikeshedding** trap if you aren't careful, but don't be scared! This is where we can thank our lazy brains for the way they summarize and simplify things; in this case, via the peak-end rule.

The good news is that not all experience points are created equal. You already know that priming and properly drawing people in matters to ensure there is an experience to evaluate. Beyond that, there are two points to keep in mind: the peak and the end.[64]

The peak and the end can be a single point: You can end on a high note, like a fireworks display—or something can be such a bad experience that the customer terminates their relationship with you. So, as you can see, there will be both positive and negative peaks.

We like to think that we do a thorough evaluation of an experience, but really think about it. If I ask you about your last trip, would you evaluate every single moment? Would you assign numerical values to each aspect—like comfort, stress, and food—then compare them? If so, how would you rate the importance of each category and convert "points" from one to the next? And in that case, what would be the conversion between each category? Is it two stress points for every food point or three?

Of course, you don't do this! It would take too much time and energy for minimal gain. Instead, our brains find the most prominent peak (positive or negative) and the most recent experience (the end) and use those data points to answer the question, "How was it?"

For your experience (regardless of business type), you need to:

- Plot out the main points in the journey (good news, you should have already done this in Part II).

- Take a good, hard look at what it is really like. There is no value in glossing over a bad experience here. Be brutally honest and rank each experience point from -10 to +10.

- Focus your effort first to remove any negative peaks (especially if they are the most extreme number).

- Bolster up your positive peaks.

- Make sure the end is as good as it can be.

Know the True End

If you were doing an experience journey for Disneyland, when would you say the experience ends? Is it when the guest leaves the park? That's what most of us might think, but the Disney team knew better. Decades ago, they realized the experience ended when people would get home, have their film developed, and look back at the pictures. So, they worked with Kodak to paint the park in the colors that would look best on Kodak paper, to help ensure the best possible end to the Disneyland experience.[65] Today, we might be posting to Instagram or TikTok (or reviewing on our phones) instead of waiting for film to develop, but that experience still extends beyond the gates of the park.

For your company, take some time to understand the journey and where it ends. Perhaps you use a third party for delivery—what kind of experience do they provide? Is it aligned with your brand and what you represent?

Once you have identified the "end" of the journey—plot out what happens one step beyond that. Is that your true end?

SURPRISE AND DELIGHT

Why does removing the negative peaks matter? Why do you need to care about the whole experience first before encouraging people to start sharing about you on social media? It's because people expect a smooth and easy experience with companies these days. When things go wrong, they tend to get mad. The degree of anger can vary (though it often seems out of proportion to the degree of your believed misstep), and when they get upset, they feel the need to vent and share... with friends and family, posting bad reviews and low star ratings, expressed via news stations and on their social media channels. This negative social proof is bad for your business, and something that is really hard to fix once it is already out there. It will take a lot more positive reviews to balance out that single negative one. How many?

We don't know for sure (and the algorithms are always changing), but a fascinating article in *Inc.* estimates that because people are much less likely to leave positive reviews than negative ones (they say one in ten happy customers will leave a positive review) and they say you need four five-star reviews to balance out a single one-star review…that adds up to a recommended forty great experiences to outweigh that single bad review.[66] Yikes! And, because ratings and reviews live forever, they can continue to do damage even years after you have fixed whatever issue they are complaining about. So, while you don't need to remove everything bad that could possibly happen, if you can eliminate the biggest negatives and simplify your experience a bit before investing in asking for social proof, you will be in a much better spot than what could happen if you get a bunch of negative reviews to kick things off.

When it comes to propping up positive peaks, your best investment will be in incorporating **surprise and delight**. Delightful experiences are those we can't help but share, whether it is with our best friend or across social media. Moments of true delight increase the likelihood that more people will leave more positive reviews, ratings, and social posts, or talk about you with friends. So, create moments of delight that people can't help but share.

What does this look like for brands?

The key to delight is the unexpected.[67] When anything is expected, the most we can get is satisfaction (and that isn't post-worthy). I mean, have you ever felt inclined to share that you saw some chips in the vending machine, put in the money for them, and they fell as expected (and tasted as expected)? Of course not. But what about when the chips get stuck in the vending machine? That leads to outrage and something worth complaining about to anyone who will listen. What about when you get a "bonus" snack when two bags of chips fall instead of the one you paid for? Delightful! You might even brag about it to your friends or strangers because you are excited by the unexpected win.

The brain chemical at the root of this is **dopamine**, which you learned a bit about earlier. We get a certain amount of dopamine (a chemical the brain likes) when we anticipate something. If you get what you expected, then you got the dopamine the brain was planning on, and it isn't worth sharing about. If you are expecting (for very simplified, rounded numbers that are not at all how the chemicals are calculated in the brain) five dopamine points and you don't get your chips? How far would your anger skew your negative response? One? Zero? Negative Five? If you get two bags of chips (and the extra anticipation of watching and waiting to see if those bonus chips will actually land!?!), you get seven or eight or ten dopamine points, which is delightful. If it is unexpected enough and delightful enough, it can lead to an experience people can't help but share about.

Remember: The key is in the unexpected.

Whatever you design can't be something that is always there or available to everyone or so common that it becomes expected. This can be hard when you want to be fair to everyone, but take solace in knowing that people love an opportunity to win things or a surprise shout-out where they hear their name, or anything like that. In case you need some inspiration, here is my favorite surprise and delight example from the world of celebrity endorsements:

You may not know this, but internationally renowned singer-songwriter Ed Sheeran is a huge fan of Heinz ketchup. He even has a tattoo of their iconic label on his arm. And because Ed is vocal about his love for Heinz, his fans know it. The brand has said that a third of their Instagram posts tag or mention Ed. (Hello, social proof!) Taking advantage of this for their 150-year anniversary, Heinz partnered with Sheeran to create Edchup—a modified label for a limited time (remember this when we get to the **scarcity** section) where the tomato in the graphic had leafy hair and glasses to look like Ed—and the internet loved it. The really interesting thing is that Heinz didn't reach out to Ed, *he pitched them* in a post on Instagram. The surprise and delight they provided was first for Ed (he called this #TheDreamThatKeepsOnGiving), and then for his fans, and then the masses. Because he was delighted, he shared about it in a really authentic way that resonated with the world.[68]

Some other examples that don't require an international superstar, custom labeling, and a 150th-anniversary campaign include:

- Zappos regularly surprises people with early delivery of their shoes (especially on a first order), so those new kicks you are so excited about show up the next day instead of in three or five. It isn't on every order (because that would be expected), but it is a fun and delightful experience when you get them early.

- Truvia sweetener packets have kind, clever messages on each one like, "Hello sweetness" and "Today's a good day for a good day" that are unexpected and make you smile. The surprise comes when you pull out a packet, not knowing what message you will get. Similarly, Bubly water adds phrases like "Hiii," "Hey you," and "Yo" at the tab, making opening each can a small, delightful surprise. And how about the facts under Snapple caps? Same concept.

- Pret A Manger has a program where every employee has to give away a certain amount of free hot drinks and food each week. They get to decide who they give it to and when, which keeps it a surprise (unlike a punch card system or other loyalty program that is more expected). And, as a bonus, because people typically don't give free stuff to people who are rude, this is more likely to encourage kind customers who are more loyal and want to come back because of this gift (i.e., **reciprocity**), and the staff feels empowered, so it really is a win all the way around.[69]

  Brainy Tip: What I really love about this example is that it shows how you can incorporate surprise and delight in a way that doesn't feel expected, even in a more formalized program. By giving staff an amount of free stuff they have to give out every week (whether it is assigned as a number of items or a total dollar amount of gift value), it makes it easy to track and ensure it is happening, but because employees get to give them out whenever they feel like, it is random and still a surprise.

- When Robert Cialdini was on *The Brainy Business* podcast, he gave a powerful example from a time when he was presenting on his principles of persuasion at a hotel and conference center. The hotel manager shared a story about a woman who wanted to play tennis with her kids but was disappointed when there weren't enough youth rackets available at the time she had allotted to play with them. She mentioned it to the staff, and they (unbeknownst to her) sent someone to go buy two more rackets from the local store and delivered them to her within fifteen minutes. She was overjoyed by the experience; she later told the manager that she was so impressed she had booked her entire extended family to come back and stay for the fourth of July weekend.[70]

Brainy Tip: it is important to note that this would not have even been a blip on the radar if the hotel had enough of the youth rackets available when they went to play. This delightful experience came from resolving a negative experience quickly and in an unexpectedly positive way that someone can't help but share about. Remember that while you don't want negative experiences, they don't have to be the end when they happen. If you act quickly, they can become fantastic opportunities for your business to create amazing positive peaks.

How might your brand incorporate surprise and delight and the peak-end rule into your optimized experience? Enjoy the opportunity to get creative and have some fun coming up with ideas!

LOSS AVERSION

As you've already heard from me in this book, humans are loss averse. We don't like the idea of missing out (FOMO, or "fear of missing out"). This is so common that the level to which we don't like it has been quantified. Many studies in very different areas have found that it takes double the joy felt by a gain to equal the pain felt by a loss. So, if you lost $20, I would need to give you $40 for it to feel the same.

TASK: GET THE BRAIN TO TAKE OWNERSHIP

The human brain has a fascinating tendency to feel a sense of ownership over things very quickly. This phenomenon, beneficial for companies, is where people feel a sense of attachment or possession over a product or service even before they've bought it or consciously considered buying it. For example, test-driving a car can instill a feeling of ownership, making you more likely to purchase. I always think about the seagulls in *Finding Nemo* and how they constantly shout, "Mine! Mine! Mine!" Our brains are doing that constantly.

Helping someone to see themselves as owning whatever you are selling, whether it is test-driving a car, showing an unboxing video, or saying, "Imagine you're walking down the street..." can trigger this in the brain.

QUALITY BRANDS: GO DEEPER—BE PART OF THEIR IDENTITY

As you consider your buying experience, I challenge you to think beyond the idea of trying something once. Instead, lean in on all that work you did to determine what your company represents, what your customer values, and where those two things overlap. This is important because it allows you to be more than just a product or service they have or use sometimes—you can be part of their identity. In his insightful book, *For the Culture*, Marcus Collins expands on our relationship with brands. He explains that as consumers, we often tie our identities to brands we admire, with the highest form resulting in a congregation of sorts. It's not just about occasional usage; it becomes an integral part of our identity. Whether it's being a member of the BeyHive (the fan club for Beyoncé, which was started by the fans themselves) or supporting the Brooklyn Nets by buying gear before the team even arrived.[71] When brands become part of our identity, we buy to uphold that version of ourselves. And because the buyer is loss averse, they want to maintain that vision of who they are. Building on this idea, consider the following insight Jonah Berger shared in *Magic Words* about the power of switching from a verb to a noun and what that means for identities.[72]

Consider this sentence: "Mary likes to run."

Now, we turn that verb to a noun: "Mary is a runner."

Just as we perceive Mary as being more committed to running in the second sentence, customers show greater commitment and loyalty when they identify with a brand by saying, "I'm a Nike person" versus "I'm wearing Nikes."

Make your brand part of someone's "I am…" statement to become part of their habits, identity, and natural buying choice.

While creating a brand identity is crucial, sensory experiences also play a significant role in brand loyalty. Just like with **priming**, all the senses are important for triggering these reactions. That being said, touch is a particularly powerful sense when it comes to perceived ownership.[73] Think about the allure of a plush, velvety throw pillow in a furniture store. Don't you feel an irresistible urge to reach out and touch it? Know that once you (or your buyer) *do* touch the thing, the brain's sense of perceived ownership is activated as well.

Interestingly, your brand can leverage the power of touch even when someone can't physically touch the item. Our eyes are our most powerful sense; they contain 70 percent of our sense receptors and have a massive influence on buyers.[74] This is why unboxing videos, virtual mock-ups, or watching a chef take a bite of the dish and seeing the expression of satisfaction on their face all have such a great impact. We also have **mirror neurons** that help us experience through others—those mirror neurons light up as if we were the ones taking the bite, even if we are just watching a video.[75] So, invest in good lighting and descriptions to help engage potential buyers in a way that nudges their brain to take ownership.

VALUE BRANDS: GO FOR FOMO

Now, let's shift our focus to value brands. While they can also benefit from being part of their customer's identity, you are better served by investing your loss aversion focus into creating FOMO (or the fear of missing out). We will get into more detail on this in the **scarcity** section, but know that short-term deals, limited quantities, special editions, flash sales, while supplies last messages, and the like are your best path to incorporating loss aversion with your customers. **Framing** (more on this later in the chapter as well) your message in terms of its potential loss to encourage quicker buying will make a huge difference in your conversions.

TWO MORE LOSS AVERSION CONSIDERATIONS

There are two additional things I want you to keep in mind when it comes to loss aversion. First is not to promise your customers something you can't deliver on. This is why you underpromise and overdeliver instead of the other way around (you get the benefit of surprise and delight instead of the rage of loss aversion).

The second lesson is to keep this in mind as you discontinue items or remove old features. That being said, this may not come up in the way you think. Yes, people may not like losing things, but that can also help to energize your customer base and boost engagement. For example, when New Coke was announced in 1985, thousands of faithful customers wrote and called in to the company. It was up to 1,500 calls a day (over the usual 400).[76] Even though taste tests showed people preferred the new flavor, the idea of losing their beloved soda was too much to bear. It only took three months for what is now known as Coca-Cola Classic to return to shelves (and hearts). They are far from the only example. When the Concorde (which provided rapid flights across the Atlantic) announced it was going to end operations because of empty flights—it sold out. When Crayola announces the retirement of colors, crayon lovers from around the world always come out of the woodwork to share their thoughts.

It is generally not a good idea to hold onto items that are losing you money or that people don't buy anymore. So, don't be afraid of letting things go. That being said, you need to prepare for the potential backlash you might get from this. What will you do when people complain? Is there something to provide to help ease the pain until the change is permanent? And then there's the side many forget to consider: What value might there be in the increased chatter and press (a **social proof** opportunity)? People may buy more in the moments when something is announced as going away, so be prepared for that. (Be aware the surge is usually temporary, so don't immediately reverse course when customers react this way.)

Even though your conscious brain will tell you losing things is bad and should be avoided, it is actually incredibly motivating and great for energizing your buyers. So, don't be afraid to incorporate this into your buying and pricing strategy. Whatever you do, just be sure you aren't using it as a scheme to artificially influence action.

RECIPROCITY

When humans are given a gift, even a small one, they feel compelled to give something back—even when they don't realize it. Consider going out to eat and being given a mint with the check. Does this impact your tips? Most people would say it doesn't, but the research says otherwise.

Giving a single mint with the check has been shown to increase tips by 3 percent.[77] Giving two mints didn't just double the tips—they went up 14 percent! This of course isn't an endless growth curve; giving forty-five mints doesn't mean someone will tip more than their bill. However, there *is* something that increased tips even more than the mints on their own.

When the waiter dropped off the check with a single mint and started to walk away, but then stopped, turned back, and said, "You know what? For you nice people, here's an extra mint," tips skyrocketed up 23 percent.

TASK: FIND WAYS TO GIVE GENEROUSLY

Having understood the concept of reciprocity, it's now your task to find ways to give generously. Yes, you can see a positive increase from the right free giveaway (which costs you money, but you gain it back multiple times over) like these mints. For a restaurant, the cost of the mints and an extra second of the server's time is far less than the value generated by the tip increase. (For example, in the priming stories early in the chapter, luxury brands are able to invest in their own champagne or other custom free gifts because their customers give back many, many times over with their purchases. They still make plenty of money even with these giveaways—and more by including them than they would make without them.)

But whether you are a value or quality brand, your gift doesn't always have to be a monetary investment. Sometimes, gestures that cost nothing but time can be equally effective, if not more so.

Consider that example with the mints again. Sure, it is the mint—but it is also the moment of kindness. The thoughtful interaction made more of a difference than the mints did on their own. In many cases, you don't even need the mints. Writing a little personalized note on the check has also been shown to increase tips and is free.[78]

Kindness is a gift that breeds loyalty.

The following chapter talks more in depth about creating great lead magnets—a free download, tip sheet, FAQ, insider newsletter, and any other smattering of ways you can give someone awesome content in exchange for an email address. These are all an act of reciprocity and increase the likelihood that someone will want to "give back" by buying from you in the future.

Find ways that you and your team can give often and give generously. Share other people's content on social media. Tag people in your posts. Do collaborations with up-and-coming talent. Feature your customers and their businesses. Create amazing content and give it away for free—not all your content and not your best stuff, but something that will give a quick win and make them realize your expertise. Great, ongoing content keeps you top of mind. Thoughtful freebies that weave into your overall strategy make people wonder, "Wow! If this is the free stuff, I can't wait to see the value I'll get when I buy." Again, you need to find the right balance for you and your brand, but don't be afraid to give generously and often.

And don't be afraid to let your customers be part of the brand they love (as this helps with creating that shared identity). Remember the **IKEA effect**, where people place a disproportionately high value on products they partially created or assembled. In other words, we tend to value things more when we've had a hand in creating them. Where can you give your customers a chance to help shape the brand?

Subaru has created an opportunity for their customers to become ambassadors for their brand.[79] According to the Subaru website, these ambassadors are "an exclusive group of energetic individuals who volunteer their passion and enthusiasm to spread the word about Subaru to help shape the future of the brand." The company supplies them "with the latest information and branded gear to share throughout their journeys." Rent The Runway has a similar ambassador program for people with sizeable social followings who use their service.

Wow.

Can you see the social proof layering here? And the best part is, this is a huge win for both sides. As a brand, you get people who volunteer to promote you to their audiences. You get feedback from your most devoted customers in a way that increases the likelihood they will stay loyal, and the "cost" is giving them some merch and insights (that help propel your brand forward and help it be seen by more people without having to pay extra salaries and health benefits). They get to feel special—a part of the brand they love so much—and potentially get some free stuff. (And in the case of Subaru, a few free shirts and hats are nothing compared to the cost of buying cars, so it is clearly a win for the company.) Opening your brand to customers can be scary, but when done right, it pays back many times over.

As we wrap up our discussion on reciprocity, it's important to touch upon one last aspect—transparency. Being honest and open with your customers is a great gift you can give them. This might be showing behind-the-scenes footage, explaining the thought process that made your brand what it is, or a whole host of other things. Take, for instance, the rising popularity of branded podcasts. Notable brands like Dior, Expedia, REI, and Google, among others, are offering audiences a glimpse behind the scenes.[80] We love to know how things are made and what is really happening at our favorite brands, so even sharing insights derived from what your company does behind closed doors could have a massive audience who would be grateful to receive them (and, of course, this helps with social proof, priming, and loss aversion as well).

Your content could cover a range of topics, not just what is happening around the office. For instance, OnStar, the subsidiary of GM which offers navigation and emergency automatic crash response, has taken an innovative approach with their podcast *Tell Me What Happened.* Their website says the show "chronicles harrowing moments when people are forced to rely on the kindness and bravery of others. True stories of real people stepping up for each other and highlighting the importance of genuine connections during a crisis." What an amazing way to create content that people want to listen to that is intricately tied to what your brand does (and that I am also sure makes OnStar a hero at least in part in each story).[81] I am by no means recommending that everyone go out and start a podcast (trust me, they are a *lot* of work), but finding a way to connect with your customers outside of your normal course of business can be a gift they value, which can then pay dividends from their wallets later on.

Lastly, but perhaps most importantly, every brand can and should offer the gift of clear communication. It's a fundamental aspect we've touched upon throughout this discussion, and its importance cannot be overstated. Make the buying process easy and straightforward. Have an easy path to get problems resolved. Let your customers know you care and that you've thought about them when building your brand. These types of steps increase loyalty among buyers, and everyone can incorporate them.

SCARCITY

We have discussed the concept of scarcity extensively in this book, observing its use in companies like Supreme, Starbucks, Costco, Serendipity3, and eBay. This is because in the human brain, scarcity means value. And all brands—whether you have categorized yours as being focused on value or on quality—still need to care about value because we (typically) don't buy things we don't value in one way or another. So, scarcity applies to everyone. However, each business type can focus on a different area of applying scarcity to have the greatest impact. For instance, a limited-edition clothing brand might create scarcity by offering a small batch of unique designs, while an event company could use time-based scarcity by selling tickets within a tight timeframe.

TASK: FIND AND INCORPORATE YOUR SCARCITY

While it might seem that all scarcity is the same, as Mindy Weinstein outlined in her book, *The Power of Scarcity*, there are actually four different types to consider in your marketing. Scarcity can be based on **time** ("today only," "flash sale," and special coupons), **demand** ("sold out"), **supply** (limited quantities, small batch production, high-quality items that are sustainably sourced), and/or **limited editions** (holiday prints, nostalgic colors).[82]

Incorporating a message like, "Only five left in stock" can trigger a sense of social proof, which builds on our herding instincts, as well as loss aversion.

This is essentially tripling down on the power of behavioral economics to encourage your buyer to act.

What I really love about the four categories of scarcity is that it makes it so there is a true version of scarcity for every brand to incorporate. So, where do you start? Here is my breakdown of what each type of brand should focus on, in order:

Value Brands	Quality Brands
• Time	• Supply
• Demand	• Demand
• Limited Editions	• Limited Editions

As you can see, both can leverage demand scarcity and limited editions to garner buzz and take advantage of social proof. In the case of a quality brand, showcasing the demand scarcity reinforces their limited quantities (supply scarcity) and exclusivity. For a value brand, demand scarcity gets people excited and reinforces the time-based tactics, so your customers are even more loss averse and ready to jump on board because everyone else is too, and you don't want to miss out when you know all your friends (and their friends) will have this.

So, the way I recommend you approach this is to focus on the first item in your category with a mindset of how demand scarcity can keep fueling that machine. If you ever want to do a limited edition, it can be a great strategy to encourage some additional scarcity outside of your standard model (in a way that can also generate buzz and increased social proof when done right).

It's important to address a trend I've noticed among some companies and influencers—creating *false scarcity* to increase sales. This might be by putting an artificial limit on the available quantity to boost sales (so that the program is written to just start the countdown over again once the sales reach zero) or having items on sale "today only" every day.

Please, please, please do not do this.

With all the categories and types of scarcity out there, you can find a version that works with your customer's values and their brain's tendencies as well as your brand type—*and* is honest. Not every version works for every brand, and you don't need to do them all. Find the versions of scarcity that work for you and test them out—both with the messages you use and where you place them.

Whatever true scarcity you choose to feature for your business, know that you aren't limited to just one at a time or one way of showcasing scarcity. If you have the resources to do it well, you can do multiple different ones at once. If you don't have the resources, keep it simpler and do less things so they are done well. (Remember, overarching experience is always at the heart of whether or not someone chooses to buy!) And whatever you do, make sure it is easy to understand and take action. You don't want so many offers and promotions and scarcity messages out there that it is overwhelming to your customer so they decide to do nothing. Less is more (in all the ways).

FRAMING

While priming needs to draw people in (and so I always say to start with it in your pricing strategy), I have often said that framing is my favorite concept and the one I believe is most important for everyone in business to master.

Remember the lesson from framing is that *how* you say something matters more than *what* you are saying. The fantastic thing about this concept is that saying the exact same thing in two different ways makes it so the brain hears it in a completely different way.

My favorite example for framing is to imagine you are at the grocery store to pick up some milk. There are two rows that are almost identical. The only difference is that one is labeled as "97% Fat Free" and "3% Fat."

Which one do you want to buy?

I've shared this simple example with thousands of people around the world. Time and time again, the overwhelming majority of people say they want the 97% Fat Free option. Logically, we know they are the same—but they *feel* entirely different. That feeling makes us want to take a different action.

Never underestimate the power of a frame (for good or bad). For your business, the tiniest shift in your framing can make a great opportunity feel like a burden. And it's important to understand that people can't tell you it was the frame. Customers may not be consciously aware of how the framing of your product influences their perception. They might dismiss your product as "too expensive," but the underlying issue may actually be that they're not convinced by the way your product is presented. In other words, the problem may be in the framing, not necessarily in the price point.

TASK: SAY IT ANOTHER WAY

More great news about testing framing—it's often completely free! You can reframe your subject lines in your emails, the call to action in your advertisement, the language in your sales team's script, the thumbnail on your social media posts, which features you focus on, and so much more. Reframing can be incorporated into various aspects of your business. For instance, consider how you handle the following: asking questions in surveys, reviewing the insights from a focus group, analyzing your customer data, thinking about your product design, and positioning the price. All of these can be framed in countless ways, some of which are more likely to appeal to your ideal customer than others.

While there are many ways you can approach framing for your company, here are eight simple reframes that can make a big difference in any business: Make it a gift, find the rhyme, say it simply, be precise, replace if with when, shift from anyone to everyone, use you, and end on a question.

Make it a gift. When buying gifts, people will often spend more and feel better about it than if they are buying things for themselves.[83] Even if your product or service isn't something that others would traditionally think of as a gift, it doesn't mean someone wouldn't want to receive it as one. When you can put the idea of a gift into the buyer's brain, it can open you up to new customers and less concern over price.

Find the rhyme. I know it seems dumb and like it shouldn't make a difference, but our brains believe rhymes are more truthful[84] and that those who communicate simply are more knowledgeable (this is why I keep harping on about that "simplicity of experience" thing). If you remember back to the cookie stories that kicked off this chapter, you may have noticed that the good cookie scenario used a rhyming phrasing ("buy three, get one free") compared to the bad scenario's clunky "buy four cookies and only pay for three of them" statement. When you can make a simple little rhyme, it can become a mantra people remember and associate with your company and/or the offer.

Say it simply. If I said to you, "The precipitation in this current month increases the likelihood that the flora in the following month will thrive and result in prominent production," your reaction would probably be something along the lines of, "Huh?" However, when I say, "April showers bring May flowers," both a rhyme and a much simpler statement, you get it, and I sound much more knowledgeable. When we feel uncertain or lack confidence, we tend to rely on big words or other tactics to prove we are smart and worth listening to. The problem with that is humans are also wired to believe that people who speak simply are smarter and more honest than those who use tons of big words.

A real depth of knowledge is required to understand what you are talking about enough so you can calmly and comfortably make it feel easy to those you are sharing it with. Invest the time to understand your experience and offers so you can share about them in a simple way. (I'll give you an exercise to help you with this in Chapter 12, "The Placement.")

Be precise. When Richard Shotton was on *The Brainy Business* podcast talking about his book *The Illusion of Choice*,[85] one of the many things we talked about was his decision to have the subhead of the book be about the "16 *and a half* psychological biases that influence what we buy." Another little trick of the brain is feeling like people are more knowledgeable when they are precise. As he said on the show, when you ask someone how old their brother is, they might say, "Forty-two, but he will be forty-three in July." When you ask how old their cousin is? Their answer is probably, "In his early forties, I think."

We like to think rounding numbers is important, but precision stands out! Instead of 10 tips, what if you had 13? Or, taking a page from Richard's book, 16½? Yes, there are points where it is great to round, like saying "over a million served," but when you say "1,243,876 happy customers and counting," it just feels different, you know?

Campaign Monitor says their emails with numbers in the subject line nearly always outperform those without, including one with a lift of 57 percent.[86] (Consider how different that statistic would have felt if I had said "nearly 60 percent" or "over half" to feel this point—and the power of framing—in action.) So, take some time to test out reframed subject lines that include numbers, especially precise ones, and see what happens!

Replace if with when. We love to say "if" in business. It has become a staple across all kinds of communication. "If you need help, let me know." "If you have questions, I'm here." "If you want to move forward, you know where to find me." *If* is a weak way to start your sentence. It implies that it might not happen. When you use *when*, on the other hand, it has an implied next step. It isn't about *if* you want to buy, but *when* the time is right. "When you need help, here's my number." "When you have a question, please ask." "When you're ready, here is the link." This simple reframe can keep prospects moving through the buying process instead of getting stuck. You won't replace every "if" with a "when," but *when* you find the strategic opportunities to do so, take advantage of them. (See what I did there?)

Shift from anyone to everyone. Another word people use far too often is "anyone." Remember, we are a herding species, so "anyone" is isolating. It is very lonely out there as an "anyone." On the other hand, "everyone" makes someone feel safe at a time that might otherwise be full of uncertainty. Here's a simple way I use this shift on the podcast. Let's say I have been interviewing a guest and want to showcase their book and remind people where to get it. Most people's natural tendency is to say something like, "If anyone wants to get a copy of Richard's book, there is a link in the show notes."

Not very compelling.

Instead, I say, "For *everyone* who can't wait to get their copy of Richard's book, there is a link in the show notes." Simple reframe, completely different feeling.

Use "you." Although I suggested shifting from "anyone" to "everyone," that doesn't mean you should avoid addressing individuals. We are trained to recognize our names and to respond to "you" more than when it isn't included. When you can include someone's name in an ad or email, consider doing that. Also, find a way to use "you" in the language. This can make it feel more real (perceived ownership) for them, triggering action. Taking the line above, we could uplevel it further by saying, "For everyone who can't wait to get their copy of Richard's book, the link to get *yours* is waiting in the show notes."

End on a question. The human brain is wired to respond to questions differently than statements. We are compelled to answer questions in a way that we simply aren't with statements.[87] If you struggle with getting ghosted in emails, look at the end of your messages. Do you end with a statement or a question? The simple shift to a question can prompt an action. It might not close out the whole process, but it can keep it moving, which is a huge win.

While it would be nice to just throw a question mark at the end of your email, it requires a little more thoughtfulness than that—often going beyond just that final sentence. Take the opportunity to step back and consider where you are in the process and what **micro-moment** comes next. Is it to get a meeting on the calendar? If so, have you made it clear what they are supposed to do and that there is a step for them to take? People might not be taking action because they are busy and missed that you are waiting on them to do something. So, simplifying the overall message is a big win (use bold text and bullet points, and cut out unnecessary stuff), and when you then end the email with a question, it can get your responses to skyrocket. Instead of saying, "When you are ready to move forward, let me know," try including some times that can work to meet and end the email with, "Which one works best for you?" or "Do any of those align with your schedule?" Even if they say, "I can't do any of those dates," they are likely to also say, "But Friday at four o'clock is available." And the ball is rolling again.

Bringing it back to the closing line of our podcast example, we can take it another step further and say, "Are you ready to get your very own copy of Richard's book? The link to get yours is in the show notes."

Hopefully, showing you how these examples continue to grow and evolve over continual reframes shows you the value of testing and trying many options. Which is "best"? It depends! The best way to know what works best for your audience is to be thoughtful before trying things (which is what Part II was all about) and then try lots of little tests. Just don't change too much at once. Only do one thing at a time to see what works.

Where should your business start with framing? I recommend reviewing the other steps throughout the "It's Not About the Cookie" framework to help guide you. As an example, loss aversion is a form of framing. How might you frame your promotion to focus on avoiding a loss instead of a potential gain? If you have determined that your biggest opportunity is in social proof, how can you frame the subject line of your email (or the page on your website or the sales pitch for your team) in a way that showcases this concept and compels the reader to take action?

As with everything in this book, framing isn't a one-and-done concept. You can constantly iterate, tweak, and test to see continual improvement. Everything is a potential learning opportunity. This email didn't convert...I wonder why? It looks like no one even opened the email, so let's reframe the subject line and try to include a number at the beginning to see what happens. Or they opened the email, but no one clicked...is the call to action clear? Maybe we should add a button instead of that text link, or perhaps we should close on a question.

Remember to do lots of little, thoughtful tests instead of throwing everything into the pot to see what happens. If you don't keep track of the changes you make, you won't know what made the difference in your results. So, in general, pick one thing at a time and test (ideally with a control version if you can so you can see the impact, like an A/B test on an email). Here are some options you can try:

- Change your subject line and leave the rest of the email the same.

- Change the image in the social media post and keep the description.

- Change the call to action.

- Switch from a text link to a button.

- Change the color of the button.

- Change the text on the button from a statement to a question.

The options are endless, so be sure you know your goals and analyze the results so you'll continue to improve, and always look back over the full "It's Not About the Cookie" framework to ensure whatever you are trying is in line with your business type and all the work you have done so far. Did you include your priming words and/or images? Have you incorporated social proof? Where is the reciprocity?

For anyone who still hasn't gotten the free checklist and virtual glossary I have created for you to help you apply this framework again and again without missing any steps, go get yours now using this QR code or by visiting *thebrainybusiness.com/pricing-book*.

[Consider my framing on that call to action—you know I thought about it! Does it make you feel like you are in the majority if you haven't gotten your checklist? Or that you are an "anyone" sitting alone if you don't have yours yet?]

Get your free Pricing Mastery checklist and virtual glossary using the QR code and at thebrainybusiness.com/pricing-book

And for everyone who is wondering, "Wait...what about my final number? How do I set my final price in a way that encourages people to buy?" Don't worry, we're almost there. The following chapters include ways to present the choice to help nudge people to select the product or service you are featuring, and how to showcase that choice in various places, including charts, written descriptions, and scripts.

Are you ready? Let's do this.

FROM THIS CHAPTER

Tasks:

- Choose your priming words and image inspiration.
- Choose up to three social proof tactics.
- Get them talking.
- Get the brain to take ownership.
- Find ways to give generously.
- Find and incorporate your scarcity.
- Say it another way.

Key Terms:

- Priming
- Herding
- Social Proof
- Loss Aversion
- Quality Brand
- Value Brand
- Micro-Moments
- Reciprocity
- Framing
- Scarcity
- Halo Effect
- Bikeshedding
- Peak-End Rule
- Surprise and Delight
- Dopamine
- Mirror Neurons
- IKEA Effect

CHAPTER 11

THE CHOICE

You now know that we all make a staggering 35,000 decisions each day, with the presentation of the choice often swaying us one way or the other. Think about the last time you stood before a restaurant menu; did the appealing description of the special make you rethink your go-to order? Given this, shouldn't we pay more attention to how we structure and present choices? Why is this critical factor so often overlooked?

The main reason is that the significance and profound impact of choice architecture isn't fully understood by many. And that goes for both your competitors and those who are providing advice on how to create your strategies. So, while everything in this book matters, the insights in *this* chapter will give you a massive edge against your competition, because while choices and their architecture are central to behavioral economics (Nobel prize winning stuff), it is also one of the key areas that others will completely skip over or undervalue.[88] That leaves an opportunity for you to be more thoughtful and stand out.

UNLOCK YOUR SUPERPOWER: CHOICE ARCHITECTURE

I see the ability to break down and analyze choices as a sort of superpower; a power you have earned with all the work you've put in throughout this book. Now I will teach you how to build on everything you've learned so

you can set yourself apart from the competition and increase the likelihood
that your best offer (which you selected in the "offer" chapter) will be
clearly seen as the best (and the easiest for people to naturally choose). We
will do this by carefully curating the items you offer alongside your best
offer, and by strategically selecting how you price and present everything
for the optimal choice.

Some may shy away from the idea of structuring choices. Those people
may think, "I don't want that kind of responsibility, can't people just decide
for themselves?"

Here's the thing: Whether you think about it in advance or not, the way
you structure the choice (whether it is alphabetical, by popularity, or at
random) impacts the decision people will make. There is no way around
being a choice architect, so isn't it better to be thoughtful about it?

I think so and hope you do too. And the best thing is that when it comes to
your pricing strategy—the opportunities presented by choice architecture
are fantastic for your business.

Why? Because even if you have struggled with getting people to buy
from you before—even if it has been difficult and it feels like everyone
complains about the price or questions whether it's the right option for
them—that doesn't mean there is anything "wrong" with your offer or
with the price you are charging. It might just be that the choice needs to
be presented differently. You now have the superpower to dissect those
choices, understand the behavior, and present the options in a different
way that is more likely to result in the action you want. Hopefully you are
excited about this process, so let's dig in!

TASK: CREATE YOUR NUDGES

For this step in your pricing process, you are going to continue working on the **micro-moments** you began working on in Part II. Now is where you get to use those insights to create the nudges for the nudgeable moments you identified.

You have already completed the first three steps in this list (if you haven't completed these yet, take a moment to do so now):

1. Consider the small steps (micro-moments) in the customer's journey

2. Identify some nudgeable moments

3. Prioritize your nudgeable moments using my Nudgeability Quadrant

Now, we get to move on to crafting that choice architecture:

4. Zoom in and out on the highest priority nudgeable moment, which you selected during the group exercise in the "offer" chapter

5. Determine the behavior you want from this moment and where/how the customer might err if not nudged

6. Create your nudge for this moment

7. Repeat steps 4–7 until all your important nudgeable moments are optimized

Let's look at each of those in more detail so you can unlock your superpower.

Step 4: Zoom in and out on the highest priority nudgeable moment. In this step, you will start by revisiting the micro-moment you chose as your top priority in the "offer" chapter and getting even more curious about it.

Let's say this moment is when someone leaves an item in their cart. According to BigCommerce, for every ten customers who add an item to their cart, seven of them don't make a purchase. Abandoned carts result in

$18 billion worth of lost sales every year.[89] Clearly, abandoned carts are a big deal, and there are some important micro-moments there. If your moment is twenty-four hours after they left the cart, yes, you want them to come back and complete the purchase, but first you need them to open your email. That is a micro-moment where your *subject line* matters. Then you need them to read the email's headline (another micro-moment), remember what they were looking at (another micro-moment), care enough to click a button (another micro-moment), and eventually complete the purchase (a step with more micro-moments).

Whatever your micro-moment is, don't just take it at face value or assume that the way you first saw it, or how the group interacted with it, or what motivated you to write it down in this way is true. Even if what you thought *is* true, it likely isn't the only truth that exists. What else may be true? How might it be false? What are you missing? When I say "zoom in and zoom out," I want you to imagine this moment is a physical object: Look at it through an imaginary camera lens that allows you to zoom in on the finest details, then zoom back out and take a few steps away from that object—what else comes into focus? Pick up your object and look at it from different angles—what hidden aspects can you shine a light on when you ask lots of questions about it?

In the case of the abandoned-cart email, you may assume that the issue was that they were concerned about the price and could need a discount to encourage them to buy—but this isn't necessarily true (and as you know, discounts aren't a good choice for every business). So...what else might be true? Perhaps they just forgot! People are busy, and there are lots of distractions in the 35,000 decisions they make per day. Is a simple reminder enough? What else could be going on that is worth testing? Make notes about all the options.

Step 5: Determine the behavior you want from this moment, and where and how the customer might err if not nudged. Now that you have thought about your micro-moment in more depth, consider what you want someone to *do* in this particular moment. In our example above with the email, you want them to open it. So, how do you nudge them to take that desired action?

A popular model used in behavioral science, known as COM-B, posits three factors needed for someone to change their behavior: Capability (the person's physical or psychological ability to enact the behavior), Opportunity (the external circumstances which make the behavior possible), and Motivation (the brain processes that energize and direct the behavior).[90] Before you move on to step six, ask yourself if the person has the capability, opportunity, and motivation to do what you want them to do in this micro-moment. If the answer is yes, make some notes about what that looks like in your case. If the answer is no, see if you have options to change that before moving forward.

For our "open the email" moment, assuming you have the right email address and aren't getting hung up in a spam filter (which is something to check), they should have the opportunity and capability to open the email— the motivation will be determined by how you tackle the next step.

Step 6: Create your nudge for this moment. Continuing with the behavior of "open the abandoned-cart email they receive twenty-four hours after leaving the website," you need to motivate them to want to open the email, and your tool for doing that is a captivating subject line. Use your tips from the last chapter (particularly the section on **framing**) to write out a list of potential subject lines:

- Include your **priming** words.
- Try some numbers.

- What if you make it a question?

- Throw in an emoji or two.

- Create some curiosity.

When I worked at an advertising agency years ago, my mentor tasked me with creating a tagline for one of our clients. He told me to spend an hour writing everything I could think of and then put my notebook away. Then, the next day, I should spend another hour and again put my notepad away. After four days (and four hours) of doing this, he said that I "might have something worth using."

I won't make you go quite that far, but it is important to take more time to think through and consider your frames—much, much more than you think you need to take. I encourage my clients to draft at least ten (preferably twenty or more) subject lines before deciding which ones to test. The rationale behind this is that it facilitates creativity and helps ensure your subject lines are as engaging and impactful as possible. Get the surface-level ideas out of the way (chances are they aren't intriguing enough to motivate the potential customer when you are competing with so much other captivating stuff) so you can get to more interesting subject lines that might actually drive the behavior you want.

Whatever your micro-moment, go to a similar depth as you craft out your nudge. Some key concepts to consider incorporating into your nudge are:

- Loss aversion

- Anchoring

- Social proof

- Scarcity

- Creating curiosity

- Surprise and delight

- Framing

Once you have your nudge outlined, set it up (ideally with a test condition so you can see how effective it is in moving you toward your desired goal).

Step 7: Repeat steps 4–7 until all your important nudgeable moments are optimized. As you saw, there are several connected micro-moments that you'll likely want to work through as you consider this full experience. "Abandoned cart" has multiple points of interaction; one of them is the email they receive twenty-four hours later (which is likely one of multiple emails you will want to send). The email itself is a journey of many micro-moments and nudges the recipient will encounter along the path. You don't have to optimize every tiny step, but there are likely more opportunities to nudge than you previously considered as "something that mattered."

This is the best part: You get to be creative and try things out that can create a great lift for your business (and hopefully, as with this email example, will have some options for automation and/or documenting processes so you don't have to start from square one every time). As you go through the process and get more practice with it, I promise it will get easier and become more intuitive; you need to do it enough to move the new behavior from your conscious to your subconscious, and that is only completed by doing it multiple times. My top advice is to frame this properly in your mind. If you see it as a chore, it will be. If you see it as a fun opportunity, it will be that too. So, whatever you do, have fun with it!

There's another benefit to having fun and being creative with your tests: Often, the "random" stuff has the biggest impact. As an example, when Stephen Wendel was on my show, he shared about an initiative to get a financial institution's customers to stop wasting money on unnecessary fees. They had multiple variations they tested out on the monthly statements: some with logical arguments, others with big buttons, and one with a cartoon of a monster eating the customer's money. Can you guess which one performed the best? That monster stood out and was most likely to change behavior.[91] So again, have fun with this! I can't wait to hear what you come up with and what you learn! (Come share it with me @thebrainybiz on social media and use #TruthAboutPricing.)

TASK: BUILD THE CHOICE BEFORE THE CHOICE

As you now know:

- Your customers each make 35,000 decisions per day.

- The bulk of those decisions are made by the subconscious using rules of thumb.

- Those rules of thumb are created based on repeated exposure and built over time.

To get your customers to choose you, it is ideal to have them interact with you enough to form a rule of thumb about *you* that says, "We like XYZ company, and when we see things from them, we engage (and buy)." If your ideal customers only hear from you when you are trying to sell them something, and they don't have multiple, repeated opportunities to "buy in" on your brand, you won't become a rule, and every sale will be an uphill battle against the subconscious.

How can you nudge them to naturally choose you more? By creating engaging content that piques their interest. This could involve educational blog posts, intriguing social media posts, or enticing email newsletters that they look forward to opening, reading, and clicking. For example, my friend Chris Rawlinson and the team at 42courses always include an "on this day" section in their Weekly Reads newsletter that has a fascinating list of curated items often going back hundreds of years.[92] I always open (and save) their emails, both for the useful behavioral content they share and because I love to review these interesting facts. This isn't a cookie-cutter style recommendation saying that everyone should include these exact facts in their newsletters. Rather, this perfectly fits the brand voice and audience (people who love to learn), so it is a great way for 42courses to get continued interaction with their current and potential customers. What aligns with your customer's interest will likely be completely different, so take some time to think about what that could look like now.

In the "customer" chapter, I had you start thinking about your lead magnet—that gift you give to someone in exchange for their email address. Once you have their email (and they have opted in via whatever standards are set in your country), you need to send consistent communication and stay on their radar.

You should also be visible in other areas (on social media, in advertisements), but consistent communication from you that encourages them to *open and engage with your brand on a regular basis* is critical for your overall buying process. Why?

Because it gets them into the habit of choosing you. Of engaging with you. *Of saying yes to you.* Of wanting to see what you have to say. Of feeling excitement when you land in their inbox. Of seeing themselves as the type of person who likes you and what you've got going on.

These tiny moments of yes are a form of **self-herding**. Remember that every interaction with your brand builds up a memory of how this person feels about you. If they "buy in" on what you are saying in your email communication, it will be much more natural to buy when the time comes. These buy-in moments are all about priming and setting the stage for what your brand is about—they are a big piece of your scent of the cookies. So, revisit your notes from the "customer" chapter and take some time now to reflect upon those insights and what you learned in the "It's Not

About the Cookie" framework (I specifically suggest looking back on the **reciprocity** section) to determine what you might share consistently that your potential customers will be delighted to engage with.

Quality Brands: Look for the things that are related to the work you do and that complement (rather than compete with) what you sell. In the last chapter, I mentioned OnStar's *Tell Me What Happened* podcast, which is all about harrowing rescues in vehicles. This is a great example of being visible in a way that aligns with what you sell, but isn't the thing you sell. Their engaging podcast reinforces the value of the brand over the year or more between the original decision to subscribe to their service and the choice to resubscribe or let it lapse. Even better, it subtly shows people again and again how others like them survived scary, real-life events (**social proof**) by having OnStar in their car. It makes it much more difficult to get rid of the service when you constantly hear stories of how it saves lives.

Value Brands: You have it a little easier because your **scarcity** promotions, deals, discounts, and other related "hacks" or tips are easy candidates for regular communication. In your case, you can probably talk all about what you have on sale and, assuming the deals are good and worth checking out, encouraging people to engage with the emails. There are of course many other ways to create an engaging, regular email as a value brand, so you should still feel free to get creative as you consider what you might be able to provide your current and potential customers to stay on their radar and continually get buy-in in between moments where it is time to buy.

TASK: CREATE A WINGMAN

It is hard for people to buy without context and points of comparison. Humans need context to know something is a deal, establish value, and buy.[93] Whether it is houses, restaurants, candy bars, potential dates, clothing, consulting packages, or anything else, tons of research and live studies have shown this again and again. Here is a quick example to show how it works:

Imagine you own a small electronics store and have decided to sell espresso machines. After extensive research, you've found the best model, one that you think customers are going to love. You price it at $149. You don't have any other espresso makers in the store, so you place it on the shelf between a microwave and a toaster. After six months and lots of lookers...it is still sitting on the shelf (with a bunch more in the back room collecting dust). What's wrong? You wonder. And whether you think you need to get out of this game or stimulate the market, you decide to sell it at a deep discount just to get it off the shelf (even though you will make little profit or possibly lose money).

$149

*When there is just one espresso machine
it can be hard to make a decision.*

While this is a common choice business owners make, it isn't the right one. *What you should have done* is gotten another espresso machine that is double the size and put it on the shelf next to the first one with a $300 price tag on it. Now that we have some context, the first machine feels like a great deal! The customer can see it is compact and will fit on their counter—making it a great introductory model.

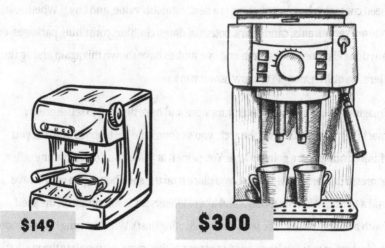

Adding a second, larger machine that is twice the price makes the first machine feel like a great deal—it is easier to decide.

While you, the business owner, would be delighted if someone bought the $300 machine, *its job is not to be purchased.* Its job is to make the best offer look good. It is the wingman of your best offer. This only works when the item is very similar and clearly worse than the thing you are actually trying to sell. (Note: "worse" doesn't need to mean that it is bad quality or anything like that, it could just be that it is "bigger" and most people want something compact for the counter, or that it is more expensive—but not a bad value for those who need it.)

To help identify what your "wingman" will be, you need to look at what makes your best offer the best. What are all the features and benefits of that offer?

Once you know that, you can compare those with the values of your customer and the type of business you are in to find the wingman. For value brands, being more expensive is likely a bad thing, but for a "quality" brand, bigger and more expensive could be the best offer. You need to know your goals as you think about how you can showcase what is best. (Thankfully, you already know that from Part II!)

Notice the prices of the espresso machines: The smaller model is listed at $149, whereas the larger model is a full $300, effectively showing what a great deal the smaller model is. This feels different than if the smaller model was $150—or if the larger model was $299.

Did you notice that the font size on the $149 model was also slightly smaller than the $300 model? There is a reason for that, which I will tell you more about later on in the chapter. For now, look at the image again and reflect upon what this difference in font size said to your brain.

For a quality brand example, imagine that you are selling bags and you want to show the value of the bigger size. That large bag could be sixteen by thirteen inches and priced at $500 (or perhaps $497 if you opted to be in a rounding down strategy). If the midsize bag in the same style is twelve by seven inches and $425, the bigger bag may feel like the best option because it is much more bag for not a lot more money.

By contrast, if you wanted the midsize bag to be the best offer, it might be $397 compared to $550 for the larger one. (If your business has decided not to round down, which is much more common and what I recommend for quality brands, I might suggest going with $400 and $555 instead.)

Of course, you need to know your numbers and do what is needed to ensure the best offer is still profitable, but adjust the numbers however you need to so it works. Play around with the options (What if we did $498 instead of $487? Does this feel like a clearer choice when the wingman is $564 instead of $550?) until you find something you want to move forward with.

Brainy Tip: You aren't required to have matching rules and markups from cost on every item you offer. Don't be afraid to have different margins on different items. You also don't need to feel confined by having everything priced in round numbers or ending in 25 or 95 or whatever else. As you saw above, I made the wingman clearly worse by moving its numbers so they were at or above the standard rounding points. That stands out to the brain when compared with the best offer, which was just *below* a rounded option. And that "clearly worse" rule of the brain is what you are looking to trigger to help make the decision as easy as possible. Play around with it, and when you get it to the point that people say, "Why would anyone pick that one?" you've made a great wingman.

SHOULD MY PRICES END IN A 5, 7, 9 OR 0?

Because I get this question all the time, I'm guessing this section might have you asking what the best number is to end your prices with. I know there are lots of opinions and advice out there where people say you "have to" end in a 7 or that a 9 is "always" best. As you hopefully saw in the examples above, context matters, including the comparison of your wingman to the best offer, so what you want someone to do is the most important thing as you finalize your prices.

This decision is a common place where people **bikeshed**, so I want to be really clear that you can choose any number you want. The main point of differentiation is for our **quality brands** (and gifts), versus our **value brands** which want to be seen as a deal, bargain, or discount.[94]

People are more likely to want to pay a whole number price (like $90) or a number just above the rounded number (like $42) for a luxury item or gift. As an example, when a camera was positioned as something to take on vacation (a luxury item), people wanted to pay more for it than when it was positioned as something you needed for work or school. Same camera, but the context mattered for determining value.[95]

For the quality brands, in general, stick with whole numbers on your pricing ($450 or $455 instead of $449 or $457 or $459). Hopefully you can feel the difference when you see those numbers and see why the last three prices are priming for a very different experience with the brand than the first two—one you don't want your buyer to have.

If you are a value brand or want your price to be associated with a bargain or deal of any kind, you should be *below* the whole number. Once you have made the choice to be a bargain, it doesn't really matter if you are $89, $88, $87, $86, or $85. That can be to your preference. (I don't recommend you price your best offer at $81, $82, $83, or $84 because it is more likely to have the opposite effect and remove the value of it feeling like a bargain.) To choose your number, test it out and determine what feels good to you. Whatever resonates with you the most and therefore feels intuitive is a great choice.

And of course, keep in mind which item is your wingman and which is your best offer to set those numbers up appropriately. The best offer needs to clearly feel like the best, and the wingman should help that best offer look good. As with everything, confidence is the most important thing, so choose a number and go with it. Also, when you are unsure—test it out! Pricing isn't forever, so you always have an option to try something else later if this isn't getting the results you want after a reasonable period of time.

Brainy Tip: Look to the left. If you do choose to go with a discounted price, rounding down is most effective when the leftmost number goes down. So, rounding down from $500 to $499 feels more significant than if you go from $2,500 to $2,499. It still matters, but it doesn't hit us quite as powerfully as when the number all the way to the left goes down, as you can see in the perceived difference between $2,000 and $1,999. If you have to be just above a milestone number—let's say your expenses make it so $2,025 is the absolute least you can price your item and still make money—as a value brand, you will often be better off increasing the price just a bit so it doesn't feel like you are gouging people for every penny. Sometimes, $2,099 or $2,249 may feel like a better deal than $2,025, even though the number is higher.

A NOTE FOR SERVICE-BASED BUSINESSES

If you sell services, you may be feeling like you don't have as many options for incorporating a "wingman" as in these product-based examples I've showcased so far in this chapter. Thankfully, that's not true! There are tons of options for you. Here's my tried-and-true process for service-based businesses to use to find their wingman: Whatever your best offer is, think about the most outlandish version of it.

This is something that most clients don't need, but you would love to provide (and this is important, because you might be surprised by how many people will choose this when you start offering it, so you don't want it built on work you are going to hate). As an example, your wingman offer might include lots of handholding and work done for your client (instead of them doing it themselves), an option that would make it prohibitively expensive for most. Still, some could want it if they value the time over the expense. Much like the $300 espresso machine, this option's job isn't to be sold, but if someone does opt into this more expensive option, you should still be delighted to sell it.

If you are a graphic designer, you may have a rebranding package that includes creating a new logo and some other key assets for the client for $2,400. This covers two revisions and a few meetings and includes the minimum number of logo options: black, white, two-color, vertical, and horizontal.

Now, let's say you create a branding package that includes a more in-depth dive into the background to come up with your client's new logo. For this package, you do up to ten revisions and will create an animated version of the logo that can be used on social media. Instead of limiting it to two colors, they can have up to four. You also agree to promote the logo to your social following and feature their brand on your website or send out a press release. Plus, you give them some PowerPoint and social media templates and a custom color palette with a brand style guide. This option is $7,500.

It is more than what most people need, but it would be an excellent project for those who want it. And you can have some a la carte pricing for people who want the standard package but also want to add in a PowerPoint template or an animated logo. Win-win!

Now, did you notice a funny little thing that happened when we added in the second price? When you first read about the logo project, $2,400 might have felt expensive. But once we added in a $7,500 option? It magically feels so much smaller! This is because of our next tactic, which builds on the wingman strategy: creating a high anchor.

TASK: SET YOUR ANCHORS

I love anchoring because it is such a simple, yet counterintuitive, concept—definitely another one of those weird brain tricks where the conscious brain gets everything totally backward. For the vast majority of people, when creating and presenting offers, they will start low and build up to the biggest, most expensive offer.

This is the wrong approach.

You need the high anchor to help the next number feel smaller by comparison (again, wingman). Taking this further, the main thing you want to sell should not be the most expensive thing you offer. You need to create something bigger to help ease the buying process (see previous section).

In the case of the espresso machine, the $300 option created a high anchor. If you are that graphic designer with the two branding packages, you want to introduce your wingman (which is also a high anchor) *first* so it makes the best offer feel lower by comparison, and thus easier to move forward with. The way you **frame** and present the offer is everything in helping someone make the choice. To show you what I mean, consider these two examples:

Scenario 1: "I'm so glad you are interested in a branding package with us. We have a package for $2,400 that is just two colors and no more than two revisions. And I know you might be thinking, $2,400 for a logo? That's super expensive! But…it really isn't when you consider our other options. We have an even bigger package that is $7,500. It has lots of stuff you probably don't want or need, but it can be a good fit for some people… Oh… and we also have a la carte options if you aren't ready to jump into a full big project like this…"

Yikes.

If that person gets anything from you, it is probably going to be an a la carte option that you don't actually want to sell them. If your sales pitches go something like this, don't despair! You have such a great opportunity to reframe how you speak about and present the choice in a way that will make it so people feel more comfortable buying from you, without you having to change your pricing at all. Consider this second experience:

Scenario 2: "I'm so glad you want to get a branding package with us. The Polished Package includes a beautiful four-color logo that we ensure is perfect for you with up to ten revisions. You also get an animated version, which is great if you do a lot of videos and presentations and want to really leave a lasting impression on your customers. We also create custom templates for your PowerPoints, social media, and more. You get all that custom created for you for just $7,500. We also have our Essentials Package, which has just that, the essentials that most businesses need from their branding: a two-color logo custom created for you with up to two revisions, and other key brand assets for just $2,400. Which of these packages seems like the best fit for your business?"

Starting with that high anchor and incorporating some key reframes made it so $2,400 seems like a great deal (and showcased some of the awesome add-ons from the larger package as well so they may also be interested in adding on items on top of their $2,400 investment). We will get into scripts, charts, and other options for presenting your pricing in the next chapter, but hopefully this example will get your wheels turning about what your wingman as a high anchor can look like, as well as why the order you present items in (and how confident you are when speaking about them) matters.

CONSIDER A BUNDLE

Contrary to popular belief, you do not have to include a discount to justify a bundle. The appeal of convenience and perceived value can often be enough. Sometimes people will even pay more for the benefit of having their items pre-bundled. Seriously, check out bundles of kids' party supplies on Amazon. Often, you would save money by searching for and buying them separately. Most people don't take the time to do that and are happy to pay whatever the price is. If they didn't like that option, they could do their individual searches and add things to the cart one at a time. I don't know about you, but for me (and most people), saving those five to ten (or thirty) minutes is worth three bucks.

Your bundle can just be a combination of the things you already offer (or two of whatever the item is you are looking to sell), or you can create something new. Consider this scenario for a company that sells DIY training courses for small business owners. They have three courses, which are complementary (i.e., you could benefit from doing all three, but they can also stand alone). Here is what their current pricing looks like:

Version A:

- Entrepreneurship Basics Course: $600

- Pitching Your Business Course: $750

- Optimizing Your Productivity Course: $900

If you were the customer, which course stood out to you as the one you might want to buy? Now what if I told you this business is most interested in selling the Optimizing Your Productivity Course—did that line up with what felt like the best option to you as the customer? Probably not, because you were anchored on the lowest price first ($600) so $900 feels really expensive in comparison. You as the buyer will probably rationalize that you will start with the Entrepreneurship Basics and assume that if you like that course, you might try another one later.

(Note that it feels like an introductory course because it is listed first and is the only option with the word "Basics" in the title, compounding the problem.)

Since this isn't what the business wants people to do, let's try a simple flip and reorder the options to see how that feels.

Version B:

- Optimizing Your Productivity Course: $900
- Pitching Your Business Course: $750
- Entrepreneurship Basics Course: $600

How about now? I'm guessing you are more open to the $900 option, and when presented this way, you are likely leaning toward the middle choice: the $750 course. While this is a step in the right direction (nudging you up from the $600 course to the $750 option), it isn't all the way to where the business wants you to be. So, let's try this one more time and add a bundle to see what that does for our choices.

Version C:

- Ultimate Business Success Bundle: $2,250
- Optimizing Your Productivity Course: $900
- Pitching Your Business Course: $750
- Entrepreneurship Basics Course: $600

How about now? The $900 option looks way more appealing, doesn't it? Again, *nothing* about the products has changed (and people probably didn't even realize they could buy multiple courses together before), so this may even result in some sales that are significantly more than the company initially imagined. And as you see here, I presented it without any sort of discount. Did you even notice that as you evaluated the options? Probably not. Even a token benefit, like rounding it down to $2,000, could help boost the bundle sales.

But now the question is...which is the best offer that you *really* want to sell? Has it become the bundle? If so, rounding that down could make sense. For value brands who round down, what happens if the bundle is $1,999 instead of $2,000? Or even $1,750 (remember, these are DIY courses and the business expends little to no effort per user, which could make the bundle become the clearly best offer and a win-win for both the business and the customer). As always, when you go to apply these insights into your business, it is important to know your goals and company type so you can leverage your high anchor and wingman to make the best choice easy.

Should I Include the Fees or Add Them Later?

Once, I tried to buy a razor holder from a small business website. The item was $6.99, and I wanted it because it would solve a problem for me. I clicked buy—and saw there was an additional shipping fee of $3.99. This item is tiny and can't weigh more than a couple of ounces; it could easily ship in a regular envelope with a few stamps. I spent nearly *three weeks agonizing* over whether or not I should buy this thing, revisiting the site and viewing the cart, debating whether I should find it on Amazon, and even asking my husband if he thought it was worth it.

Here's the thing: If it had been $10.98 with free shipping, I would have bought it immediately (and excitedly awaited its arrival). Instead, the entire brand is tainted by this bad experience.

Think about this as a consumer. Is there anything worse than being anchored on one price and then finding out the "real" price is higher, sometimes almost double what you were mentally prepared for? It is a negative surprise that can feel like a bait and switch. That can result in outrage (instead of the much-preferred surprise and delight) and unhappy would-have-been customers telling anyone they can to avoid buying from you as well.

As you consider your experience, especially if you are a quality brand, take a serious look at fees. What would it look like if they were part of the initially quoted price instead of an add-on?

One of my clients sold weighted blankets and had great success with free shipping, so this can even work with heavy items. People are generally more excited about free shipping than they are likely to notice the difference in the cost of the item. And in general, I don't recommend $1 shipping for this reason. If you can afford to do it for a dollar, there is typically enough upside in having it be free (since people love free stuff) than the income you would get from the nominal charge.

If you are a value brand, look for ways to get creative with this. Some sites have free shipping for orders over $50 or $100—which can encourage higher orders and ensure you only give this benefit when there is enough margin to make it worth your while. If your main channel is a comparison site where every dollar and penny counts, it may make sense to keep the fees separate, but I still encourage everyone to consider their options here. Don't assume you *have to* do anything—including adding fees at checkout.

Finding the price that feels good to the customer and is profitable for you becomes a win-win. So, give yourself permission to play with the numbers a bit and find what works for you to absorb those fees and leave your customers feeling happier.

WHEN RUNNING A SALE: CONSIDER MAKING THE FULL PRICE YOUR HIGH ANCHOR

One of the great benefits of running a sale is that you have a built-in high anchor from the original price, which creates a comparative value in the minds of customers.

This is another funny brain trick moment. It feels like the sale price should be big and chunky to stand out and draw the customer in. After they see that price, they can see what a great value it is by noticing the crossed out original price, which convinces them to buy now.

Let's test that theory. Take a look at the image below.

The font size on your price tags matters—perhaps differently than you think.

Which tag feels like the better deal? Did the $25 option feel smaller when it was in the smaller font? This is related to the literal associations our brains make all the time. In this case: Small font equals small price. Whether you use price tags, banners on your website, or ads on social media, try displaying the original price larger than the sale price. This sets the high anchor and enhances the perception of the discount.

TASK: CHOOSE ONE UNRELATED ITEM

When making a decision, we humans like to think we have done some due diligence—it helps to feel like you have done the work to be confident in your choice. So, while having the wingman (typically a high anchor) is critical, depending on your situation's complexity, a third offer could be needed. This third offer needs to be different enough from the best offer and wingman to help put them in a box together, while not being so different that it adds complexity and creates a **paradox of choice**.

As an example, if you were a real estate agent and you were presenting options to a potential client, you could show three options:[96]

- A colonial that needs a new roof
- A colonial in great shape
- A modern home

You, of course, know enough about the couple to know they prefer colonials to modern homes, and you believe the colonial in great shape is the best choice for them. When they have seen the homes, the modern home (your unrelated, third option) becomes a clear "no." This helps the potential buyers to feel like they've done some due diligence by seeing more than two homes. They feel like they know a little more of what is out there so they are less likely to want to shop around. Now they also have some confidence from making the first decision (of saying "no" to the modern home), which will hopefully help fuel a choice between the remaining two homes.

Unless they are looking for a fixer-upper, most people don't want to buy a house where they will immediately need to take on the massive expense of fixing the roof. And that first house raises other questions of, "What can't we see? What else could go wrong?" By comparison, the colonial in great shape is obviously better (and you can explain all the other benefits of this home to help aid their choice). When presented with this type of option, most people will choose the colonial in great shape. Some will want to see more homes, and that is okay, but you shouldn't overwhelm them with options and choices up front. That will lead to analysis paralysis and delay the choice (or nudge them to stick with their **status quo**).

What might this look like for other businesses?

JEWELRY		
Necklace	$425	Wingman, high anchor
Necklace	$289	Best offer
Earrings	$350	Unrelated (also a high anchor)
VIRTUAL CONSULTING		
Big Virtual Retainer	$8,000 per month	Wingman, high anchor
Standard Virtual Retainer	$4,500 per month	Best offer
More Expensive In-Person Option	$10,000 per day	Unrelated, very high anchor
SOFTWARE		
Extra Handholding Version (includes a team member on site for a year)	$500,000 for year one	Unrelated, high anchor
Their Perfect Solution	$320,000 for year one	Best Offer
Smaller Package Missing One of Their Most Important Features*	$300,000 for year one	Wingman, low anchor

NOTE: Use this last model with extreme care, as you only want to recommend packages that will solve the problem if they choose it, and you don't want to throw in a less expensive option that could undermine what you want them to choose. In this case, the value of their "most important feature" will be much more than the $20,000 in savings for the third package, making the perfect solution the clear best option. I've included this option to show one way your wingman can be used without always being the high anchor.

While I want everyone to consider incorporating an "unrelated third item" into their offer set, know that this task has a lot of wiggle room. Sometimes, a third option will add confusion and make the decision more difficult. Regardless of whether you think you want to offer this in your final presentation or not, I recommend you walk through the exercise to determine what your unrelated third item could be. Price it out and use it as you go through the steps in the coming chapters. And even if it feels weird to you (and like people "shouldn't" be influenced by it)—test it out. Show the offer to some people, both with and without your unrelated third item. How does the choice change? Do they decide faster when it is included, or does it add confusion? Play around with it to find what is best for your business and this specific offer.

But Melina, I've Got a Lot of Products

If you have a store or a restaurant or anything else with a lot of products that you offer, don't get scared about the prospect of having to do this for absolutely everything you sell. You can't feature everything at once (and shouldn't, as it would cause overwhelm), so something will be your priority at any given time. This can change throughout the year, of course, for seasonality or special promotions. You may also have multiple personas/target customers you are working with if you have a larger brand, so there could be many journeys and "best offers" at any given time. That is the great thing about the process in this book. You can use it again, and again, and again. It is structured enough to get a groove for how it works while remaining flexible enough to adapt to any situation.

In a virtual store, you may use your high anchor in a featured image on the home page. When they click on it, they will see their three choices in the structure outlined there. If you are a value brand, this could be a very low anchor to draw them in to see more options, some of which are more expensive.

In a physical store, you put the high anchor by the front door. When they get to the other items deeper in the store, customers can see what a great deal they are compared to that high anchor they noticed on the way in.

In a restaurant, you can put the high anchors in bold or near the top or bottom of the list so they are seen first. You can't do too many, of course, but you can do this with a few key items as you guide the eye around the menu.

What If There Is Lots of Customization Available?

Product-based businesses especially are likely to have lots of options for customization: sizes, colors, materials, custom lettering, and the like. These are great for triggering the **IKEA effect** and perceived ownership so your customer feels like they are part of the creation of their new item. However, if the architecture is off, it can feel incredibly overwhelming.

This is where the U and the S in NUDGES come in: Understanding Mapping and Structuring Complex Choices.[97] Revisit your journey notes and the nudgeable moments you thought about earlier in this chapter, and consider the most logical way to break down the choices for the customer: What comes first, second, third, and so on?

Is your ideal customer most likely to search by style or by size? By color or by material? What is the default that most people will want (and do they have an option to change that if they care about some specific feature more than others)?

For example: One of my clients makes wooden shelves that are also jewelry organizers. The most common journey is to find a design you like first and then customize it for your space. Once someone finds a design they like, they can choose the length, then the color of the wood, then the color of the metal. The default option may be based on what most people will choose (an opportunity to leverage **social proof**) or on something that is most profitable for your business, or it could be set up to showcase an item with a lot of backstock.

For someone who is selling larger pieces, the dimensions may matter most so people don't fall in love with something that is too big or too small for their space. Once they make that first decision, they can find a design and then look at customization.

As you evaluate your customers, try to give thought to their experience and don't overload them with too many decisions too early. Combine or limit choices where you can (so people don't have to make twenty-eight separate choices to pick their shelf), and always look for nudgeable moments.

Congratulations! You have selected your brainy prices and are ready to move on to how you showcase those choices based on where you are communicating them, whether it is a chart, a written (vertical) description, or something being said aloud.

Before moving on to the next chapter, you should know your best offer, its wingman, your unrelated item (even if you aren't sure you will end up using one), how you will use the high anchor, and the prices you want to use for each.

FROM THIS CHAPTER

Tasks:

- Create your nudges.
- Build the choice before the choice.
- Create a wingman.
- Set your anchors.
- Choose one unrelated item.

Key Terms:

- Choice Architecture
- Best Offer
- Wingman
- Nudges/Nudgeability
- Framing
- Priming
- Micro-Moments
- Reciprocity
- Quality Brands
- Value Brands
- Status Quo Bias

- Loss Aversion
- Scarcity
- Social Proof
- Anchoring
- Surprise and Delight
- Habit
- Self-Herding
- Paradox of Choice
- IKEA Effect
- Understand Mapping
- Structure Complex Choices

CHAPTER 12

THE PLACEMENT

At this point in your pricing journey, you have built a solid foundation and considered how to optimize your customer's choice to increase the likelihood that your best offer will be selected. That means you also have your wingman and unrelated item created, along with prices (or price ranges) for each. So, what's next? This chapter focuses on the spaces where customers are most likely to encounter your price and the best ways to present it to increase the chances they'll choose your best offer.

While there are many ways that your customer can encounter your pricing, I have found that there are three main formats most businesses need to cover their pricing presentation needs:

- Pricing chart (with your offers compared side by side)
- Written descriptions (with your offers stacked on top of each other)
- Script to be said aloud (in person, on a call, in a video, etc.)

This chapter will walk you through each placement with tips to optimize each so your best offer will always shine.

TASK: PUT IT IN A CHART

One common way we encounter pricing is in a chart. Charts are a great way to break down information into digestible chunks—so fight the urge to put too much stuff there.

Brainy Tip: Find the smallest number of words you need to use to get them to make the decision—and then stop.

When you use a chart (a sample follows on the next page), you want to put the highest-priced item—your **high anchor**—on the right. (This is assuming the language you use reads from left to right.) I know this may feel counterintuitive based on what you expect to see first. However, because people have consistently put the most expensive items on the right for years, our eyes and brains are trained to look there first. If you put your least expensive stuff over there, it will inadvertently set a low anchor.

Whatever your **best offer** is should be made really clear. It is common to have it outlined, shaded a different color, or otherwise made to stand out from the other columns. This is another good way to draw attention to your best offer and keep the eyes coming back to it no matter what else they look at on the page. (While we don't consciously realize it, our eyes scan the world around us three times per second on average,[98] so having something that keeps their attention coming back again and again is really important.) You also want to give your best offer a prominent callout for its biggest benefit. If it is your most popular item, stating that is a great way to leverage **social proof**. If it isn't, find something else that is true (best value, CEO's choice, featured product, etc.). You want to do this for the best offer for sure, but not necessarily for the other two items on your chart (since the point is to make the best offer the obvious best choice). If everything has a callout, none of them will stand out.

For each point you list in the columns, be concise and clear to ensure they are easy to read and skim, while also highlighting the best offer. Have less items listed on the lower priced offer so it is clearly less robust than the best offer.

Examining the numbers side by side like this provides the ideal opportunity to finalize your prices. Play around with the numbers until you can see that one clearly feels like the best choice. You can see that in the following chart example, I have made it so the prices of the two "other" items end in fives, with the high anchor above 100, and the best offer is rounded down to be 49 so that it stands out.

Here is my sample chart, which visually showcases what I've explained so far in this section:

CALL OUT THE BENEFIT		*MOST POPULAR*	
	Lower Priced Offer (could be a free trial)	Best Offer	High Anchor (wingman or unrelated)
Point 1: Point 2: Point 3:	Not as cool Less stuff	Great point Amazing thing So awesome!	Very good Extra stuff More than most people need
	$35/month	$49/month	$115/month

Now, try it yourself:

CALL OUT THE BENEFIT			
Point 1: Point 2: Point 3:			

Brainy Tip: Ditch the decimals. Our brains see numbers with decimal points and commas as being bigger than those without. A dollar sign (or the symbol for whatever currency you use) is also more likely to trigger the **pain of paying** than if it isn't there. Research has shown that the pain we feel when paying for things can actually resemble physical pain, so it is important to be sensitive to that.[99] Take a look at these examples of how you can list an amount and see how much bigger or smaller it feels (even when we round up as we go):

$4,987.54

$4,988

$4988

4988

This underscores the fact that even the smallest details in how you present information matter. Therefore, it's crucial to thoughtfully consider how all of this aligns with your brand and its goals.

DO I NEED TO LIST MY PRICES ON MY WEBSITE?

Short answer: No. You don't need to list your prices on your website. There are lots of companies and industries where that doesn't make sense—perhaps all your work is custom. That being said, there might be a reason to include a range of prices or a project minimum (if you have one), to reduce calls from people who will never do business with you..

Brainy tip: Beware of the inadvertent low anchor you can set if you constantly talk about project minimums, assuming you want people to invest more than that with you.

In these cases, I have also found that using smart **priming** words like "investment" can help reduce the number of calls you get that will never lead to business. *Investment* is a word that implies it will cost money, without having to come out and say, "Hey, we are pretty expensive, so don't waste our time and call unless you're serious." (That rarely goes over well.)

Even if you aren't going to list the prices out on the website, I still recommend doing this chart exercise. You may end up using it on a document you can provide to qualified leads, or in a pitch presentation. Seeing things side by side is also helpful, even just for your own thought process, so give it a try.

TASK: WRITE IT OUT

Even if you have a chart, you still have times where you need to write out a description of the products or services you are offering in a way that stacks them on top of each other (for example: a page on your website or when explaining options in an email).

When you are writing out the descriptions, incorporate lots of adjectives—especially the three priming words you selected at the beginning of Part III. As with the callouts and focus points from the last section, this definitely applies to the best offer, but may not apply to your other offers since the goal is to make the best offer the most enticing.

In general, when you are presenting offers vertically (typically in a way that requires a scroll of a mouse or the eyes), it is important for the most expensive offer to be on the top to set your high anchor. This will likely be followed by your best offer, and then your third (least expensive or otherwise unrelated) item.

The description for the best offer should be the longest one, but it shouldn't be excessively long; aim for around seventy-five to a hundred words. For context, this paragraph is eighty-seven words. This description will also feature your best, most descriptive language to help it be the most appealing. The other two options will be shorter and less opulent in their word choice—aim for them to be about fifty words each. This will help the best offer stand out to the reader as something worth reading.

If you were describing a leather item, your shorter text could read: "Durable brown leather that stays beautiful in all conditions." Your more descriptive text might say, "Buttery-soft, chocolate brown leather you can't help but touch! You'll be amazed at how this beautiful piece holds up in all conditions."

A subtle difference, but one is really pulling you in while the other is more factual. Since you want your best offer to pull them in, it gets more adjectives and descriptive language than the other options.

Brainy Tip: Ease the pain of paying. I've mentioned already that you should reduce additional fees when possible, but I know that can't always be achieved. Studies have shown that using phrases like "small $5 fee"—even though it may seem unnecessary—can actually ease the perceived pain of payment. **Priming** the buyer with the idea that this really is a small fee can help them to see it that way too.

TASK: SAY MORE WITH LESS

Even if you have a marketing department or agency you work with, I recommend you practice whittling down your language to its most brief form. As you are forced to use fewer and fewer words, the main points tend to become clearer, which helps with the **framing** tactics you learned about earlier in Part III. The language you wrote in the last section was seventy-five to a hundred words about your best offer. Your task now is to gradually step your way down to find the most important words to draw in your customer—remember your three priming words!

- Write the description in 45 to 50 words.

- Write it in 23 to 28 words.

- Write it in 10 to 12 words.

- Write it in 3 to 5 words.

Once you have completed this exercise, go back to the original seventy-five to a hundred words you wrote: Are they as clear as they should be? Do you have the right words up front to help entice the buyer? Does it end in a way that makes them excited enough to take the action to buy (or book a call or whatever the next step is)? Make some adjustments so that it is as compelling as possible. And, good news, these shorter bites are perfect for use on social media and in ad copy—win!

TASK: CREATE A SCRIPT

The last way that people commonly hear about pricing options is audibly. That could be over the phone, in a webinar, at a networking event, in a video, in a pitch meeting, and more. However you and/or your team will be talking about the offer, you need everyone to be working off a script to ensure they are saying the same thing in a way that includes all the brainy goodness you've learned in this book.

Yes, it is okay for people to put their own stamp on the conversation and say things in a way that fits their style (remember, you need them to be confident). However, there are some non-negotiables in the process, so it is a good idea to do some role-playing or observe them pitching so you can be sure they are hitting the right points. The most important pieces are ensuring that they: 1) present the items in the right order, 2) incorporate the priming words, and 3) end with a call-to-action question.

Brainy Tip: Your pitch should never end on a flat note of, "Here it is." You always want to end with a question that propels the buying process forward, like, "Which of those options sounds best for you?" or "How does that sound?"

Whatever you do, please don't say, "Does that make sense?" If you or your team include this in your language now, I highly encourage you to change it. Even though you have the best of intentions with it, this question can come off as incredibly condescending. When presented with this question as a potential buyer, your options are either to say,

"No, I'm dumb, I don't get it," or to nod along to avoid having to say you don't get it.

Instead of this phrasing, I use a reframe and ask, "Did I explain that well?" This puts the pressure back on me if something isn't clear. It has nothing to do with them, so it is easier to ask for clarification and keep the conversation moving forward.

Here are two example scripts to help you create something for your needs. These are just a jumping-off point, so feel free to edit as much as you want or need so they fit your brand voice (and that of your sales team). There are templates following each example so you can build out a script that showcases your best offer.

SERVICES EXAMPLE

"There are two main ways people work with me, and it really depends on your preference and personal style. First is in person, where we sit down for a full day and work through all the options together. That is $5,000 for the day plus travel. Other clients choose to do a series of Virtual Strategy Sessions, which are $500 dollars each. Based on our conversation, I have outlined eight to ten items right off the bat that we could work on during those sessions, so I would recommend a package for you if you go that route. Most people opt to precommit to a bundle of sessions up front because they are discounted by as much as 20 percent each. What sounds like the best option for you?"

NOW YOU TRY (SERVICES)

There are _____ main ways people work with me. First, is _____.
That is $_____. Other clients choose to _____, which is
$_____. Based on our conversation [make a recommendation and make it
clear they will get value from working with you], most people _____.
Which of these sounds like the best option for you?

PRODUCTS EXAMPLE

"We have two swing set models available. First is the Ultra Deluxe. It has a super-
fast slide, a rock wall, and two swings, which you can customize with your kids'
names and favorite colors. It is $8,000. Second is the Fantastic Fun, which also has
two swings and a fast slide, but instead of a rock wall, it has a playhouse. It comes
in three different colors and is our most popular model at only $5,999—and we
have payment plans for as little as $99 per month. Which sounds like the best fit
for your family fun?"

NOW YOU TRY (PRODUCTS)

There are __[number]__ options available. First, is _____ which features
_____. That is $_____. Other clients choose to _____, which
includes _____ and is only $_____ and [if applicable] we have payment
plans for as little as _____. Which of these sounds like the best option for you?

Speaking of Payment Plans...Should I Offer Those?

As with every option available to you in business, you never *have* to
do anything. So, if you don't want to offer payment plans—don't. If you
do, they are a great option that can help people to buy from you who

might otherwise find the cost prohibitive to do so (whether you are a **value** or **quality** business).

For some of the quality brands, it may go against your intended image to offer a payment plan. For others, it could be a great option.

Whatever you decide, you want to consider what you want most people to do when you determine how to present the options to them. If you know that most people will choose the payment plan and you are happy to have that be the way they buy from you, you can leverage the full price as your high anchor so the payment plan sounds like a great deal in comparison. (See my example in the swing set description above.)

If you are okay with offering payment plans, but would prefer for people *not* to choose them, then don't showcase them as a great option when you present the offer. In fact, you probably shouldn't mention them at all in this case when you do the initial pitch. If someone asks, "Do you have payment plans available?" you can say yes and tell them about that pricing at that time, but you are under no obligation to present it to everyone before they ask.

You are also not under any obligation to have it be the same total price as if they pay up front, or to have it split into equal payment amounts. If you need more up front to cover some sort of deposit or cost of materials or whatnot, you can absolutely charge more for that first payment. If you want to increase the price of the total by 10 or 20 percent to have a payment plan (since you are taking on the risk of them not making all the payments), you can absolutely do that too.

Whatever you choose, know why you are doing it and be able to confidently explain why it is set up that way if you ever need to—just don't overexplain or apologize for anything (especially not before they ask). If your package is $5,000 and they ask for a payment plan, you can say, "Absolutely! We offer this same package for $900 per month paid over six months. Would you like to move forward with that option?"

They may notice that the total is now $5,400 for the package instead of $5,000, but likely won't mind. And, if they do, they can pay for it up front.

Can you believe how far we've come together? *The Truth About Pricing* is almost complete. Before you move on to the final chapters, take some time to finalize your scripts, review your charts, and read back over your descriptions. Do they line up together? Have you incorporated your **priming** words throughout? Do your priming images align and evoke the right emotion for that buying moment? What about **social proof** and the other concepts from the "It's Not About the Cookie" framework? Is the customer's problem (and why this is the best solution) still clear? If so, congratulations! If not, take a moment to revisit and revise what you have so you feel confident in your pricing approach. And, for extra inspiration, the next chapter includes examples from four well-known businesses showcasing how real companies are applying these behavioral concepts.

To make sure you don't get stuck mere inches from the finish line, it is important you read all the way through the final chapter, "Back to You," which has some final insights into the psychology of your own brain and tips to give you all the pricing confidence you need to close deals left and right.

FROM THIS CHAPTER

Tasks:

- Put it in a chart.
- Write it out.
- Say more with less.
- Create a script.

Key Terms:

- Anchoring / High Anchor
- Best offer
- Wingman
- Social Proof
- Pain of Paying
- Priming
- Framing

CHAPTER 13

EXAMPLES

In this chapter, you will find four case studies to show you how the "It's Not About the Cookie" framework looks when implemented by existing, well-known businesses. The examples don't show all of the ways each business is using the framework concepts, but instead are a sampling of ideas for you to incorporate into your own business. My hope is that this will bring the framework to life and show how every approach can be successful when a company owns their business type.

These four case studies were chosen to showcase one from each category:

- Quality business type, service-based business: Serendipity3
- Quality business type, product-based business: Birkin Bag (by Hermès)
- Value business type, service-based business: Ryanair
- Value business type, product-based business: Old Navy

All right, let's kick these off by revisiting an example from early in the book—Serendipity3.

QUALITY + SERVICE: SERENDIPITY3

In case you forgot, this is our restaurant with multiple Guinness World Record holding items, including their Quintessential Grilled Cheese Sandwich, which sells for $214.

PRIMING

The PR they generate around their record-setting menu items gets people excited about the prospect of eating there. There are stories across the internet—Buzzfeed's video of people trying the Quintessential Grilled Cheese has 1.8 million views just by itself. In it, the chef doesn't just say, "I mean, you know, it's a grilled cheese...it's just way more than you usually pay for one." No, no, no.

He says, "We start with this beautiful French Pullman bread that is baked with Dom Perignon champagne" [insert sighs of delight from the Buzzfeed crew, whose anticipation and excitement are growing with every word].

He goes on, "As you can see, it's flecked with twenty-three carat edible gold. What we're going to do is take a little white truffle butter and brush the bread so when we put it in our panini press, it gets a nice, crisp, great flavor...then we're going to use the crème de la crème of cheeses, which is called Caciocavallo Podolico. This is from Podolico cattle in southern Italy, of which there are only 25,000. They graze on aromatic grasses, such as wild strawberry and licorice, and they only lactate in May and June..."[100]

There's more, but I think you get the point. The viewer is leaning in along with the lucky taste-testers. This description triggers both **dopamine** from the anticipation and **serotonin** from the status of being able to try this decadent luxury item. The story being shared over the video can also create **oxytocin** release for the viewer—it's a brain chemical bonanza! Everyone is excited to learn more, and even if you don't spring for one of their expensive items, you have been **primed** to believe all the food at Serendipity3 is made by those who handle only the best. It sets your expectations and primes your experience no matter what you order.

ANCHORING AND RELATIVITY (WINGMAN)

When patrons are anchored on a $214 sandwich, the "regular" $30 grilled cheese (or whatever they choose to charge for it) may feel more like a bargain than it would have without that high anchor. Even if you would never have ordered it, you can't unknow that it exists, and it is still priming your experience because you know it and the other record-holding items are available. The same goes for the $200 french fries and $1,000 vanilla sundae. They all provide diverse high anchors that are the wingmen to the real items they want to sell—their other ice creams, sandwiches, and sides, which are still high quality and still probably more expensive than their competition's offerings.

Another way their site uses anchoring is with a header that reads, "Get a Pint... or Three" which **nudges** people to get a little extra when they are ordering. The wording of the header might not result in everyone ordering three pints, but likely nudged more people to order two than would have otherwise, and it didn't cost them anything more to frame the message this way.

SOCIAL PROOF

For Serendipity3, being featured in all those news stories shows potential patrons that other people like them love their food. Having a waitlist of eight weeks for expensive french fries means lots of other people are trying that dish, so it feels like you should too. And, in the meantime, it might inspire you to come by to try some other items that are less extravagant (but likely still more expensive than your normal meal out).

Another interesting development I found while researching Serendipity3 for this book is that actress and singer Selena Gomez is now featured on their website as a partner with the restaurant. As you know, celebrities and influencers are one of the types of social proof I recommended for quality brands because of the status that comes from a famous name being attached to your business. In their case, it's not just that Selena likes their food and was seen eating there once—she believes in it so much she is a partner with them! This allows them to leverage her fanbase and social following, as well as the "masses" of social proof that will follow their favorite celebrity, to further grow the brand. It is important to note that their extravagantly expensive items and luxury approach are probably a big reason they were able to attract someone like Selena in the first place. She can't be attached to just any brand, but she chose them because of what it says about her brand and the image she wants to portray. This goes to show that going big can pay off big when you do it right.

LOSS AVERSION

All the delicious adjectives used to describe the Quintessential Grilled Cheese Sandwich help trigger that perceived ownership and loss aversion for Serendipity3. They also have beautiful imagery of their food in those videos and on their website that partner with priming to trigger loss aversion for potential patrons.

RECIPROCITY

Serendipity3 is giving the gift of trying extravagant delicacies you might not be able to get (or wouldn't splurge on) without the shop putting it all together. Exclusive cheeses and gold-flecked crust? What a cool opportunity that you don't want to miss out on if you get the chance.

After you have been on the site for a while, you will also see a pop-up inviting you to join their newsletter "And receive 10% off a future delicious purchase." While you know that it isn't a requirement for any business to offer a discount at any time—especially a quality one—I think this is a smart tactic from Serendipity3. The benefit is a percentage off of a meal that will still bring profit to the brand, and this can **nudge** someone to try the restaurant or order those pints of ice cream if they have been on the fence. Allowing people a little taste can generate new, loyal customers. And, if people don't buy, they don't get the discount, so in this case, I believe there is enough upside to justify the percentage-off discount here.

SCARCITY

Again, Serendipity3 has this one nailed down. If you want the special menu items, they have to be ordered days in advance. This helps to showcase the fact that they are made with very exclusive items that are hard to get (supply scarcity). They know these made-to-order items are not for everyone, and they have a great selection that is available for more ordinary visits. That said, there is a **halo effect** on the entire brand from those world-record-holding items. People can feel special by trying anything at Serendipity3—it becomes an experience that is more than just another sandwich or ice cream cone.

The partnership with Selena Gomez means they have an exclusive ice cream flavor, Selena Gomez's Cookies & Cream Remix—which is of course only available from Serendipity3. They also showcase Selena's favorites on the site, so fans can feel close to her when they choose a flavor. Remember that website pop-up inviting you to join the newsletter? It features two pints of ice cream, one of which is Selena's—smart.

FRAMING

Serendipity3's ability to frame a simple sandwich as an extraordinary culinary adventure highlights the power of perspective. By describing ordinary ingredients in luxurious terms, they elevate the entire dining experience. For this final step, I want to focus again on the way Serendipity3 talks about the ingredients and preparation of their record-holding menu items. This is framed as the most amazing, decadent, wonderful meal you will ever have. It is more than just a sandwich or a sundae—it is a moment you will remember for your entire life. Changing the frame changes the whole experience.

As an example, if they said the crust had "chunks of metal" in it, you probably wouldn't feel very excited about trying it. Saying "it's flecked with twenty-three carat edible gold" is entirely different (and yet, the same). And that special cheese? When asked if it tastes like any other cheeses we might recognize, he says it is closest to a Parmesan and manchego.

I don't know about you, but a Parmesan grilled cheese doesn't sound particularly enticing. In fact, it kind of makes me scrunch my nose in disgust without being able to control it. But the most expensive cheese in the world, made from cows who only graze on aromatic grasses like wild strawberry and licorice? I'm intrigued! I want to try that. And, because our brains tend to get what they expect (thanks to the way they filter information), if I'm excited and anticipating something amazing, I am more likely to get it.

How you say it matters. And Serendipity3 knows how to frame it.

QUALITY + PRODUCT:
BIRKIN BAG (BY HERMÈS)

If you aren't familiar with the Birkin bag from Hermès, it is widely recognized as the most exclusive and expensive handbag in the world. The design was created for actress Jane Birkin, whose bag reportedly spilled out of an overhead bin on a flight from Paris to London in 1984. Her seatmate asked why she didn't have a bag with pockets, to which she responded, "When Hermès has a bag with pockets, I will." As luck would have it, her seatmate happened to be the CEO of Hermès, and they worked together on the plane to sketch the now iconic bag on an airplane sickness bag (a not-so-glamorous beginning for such a coveted item). A year later, Birkin was presented with the first of her namesake bags, and while it took several years for demand to take off, it has been regarded as the *it* bag for decades. Some say a Birkin is a better investment than gold. What makes the Birkin so special? Let's walk through some of the smart things Hermès is doing to bring this coveted bag to its iconic status.[101]

SCARCITY

The concept at the heart of the Birkin bag's success is scarcity. Not only are these bags made from exclusive and rare materials, each one is handcrafted by an artisan who reportedly trains for over ten years before they are allowed to make a Birkin. The number of bags released each year is a closely held secret—Hermès has never disclosed the quantity they have or will make. This is supply scarcity.

And, while most everyone knows what the bag is, you can't just walk into the store to get one. They used to have exclusive waitlists, which people would be on for five years or more before getting their opportunity to purchase a bag (demand scarcity), but even those are no more. Today, acquiring a Birkin requires more than money. You must spend enough with Hermès and cultivate a good relationship with a sales associate. Only then will you be given the chance to purchase the bag. At that point, you will not be able to choose your color or size, as Hermès creates just two new colors/versions each year (limited-edition scarcity), which are rarely seen again. Instead you are expected to be grateful for whatever you get (and as far as I know, everyone is).

Those bags retail for $10,000 or more each. Anyone who wants a specific size, color, or collection can buy the item from a reseller and can expect to pay above retail. The bags are sometimes sold by auction houses like Sotheby's and Christie's, and the most expensive auctioned bag to date—one which originally retailed at $300,000—was purchased for $500,000 on the resale market.

SOCIAL PROOF

The Birkin enjoys undeniable prestige, bolstered by celebrity and influencer endorsements. This social proof manifests in the way celebrities flaunt the bag, validating its status as a luxury item. Everyone who has a Birkin wants to be seen using one, and it seems that "everyone who's anyone" has a Birkin. Victoria Beckham reportedly has over a hundred of the bags, with a total value of more than $2 million. The Kardashians, of course, have massive collections they constantly tout on social media. Martha Stewart notoriously carried one of her Birkin bags when she appeared in court, which made headlines at the time.[102] The internet is full of stories featuring celebrities and their Birkin bags.

Interestingly, that half-a-million-dollar record-breaking sale was by Vegas Dave, who says he bought it for promotion and use on social media. His post announcing the purchase has over 77,000 views and 22,000 likes, so it appears to be working.[103] Since that initial post, there have been lots of articles, chatter, and features of his milestone purchase, and he has of course used the bag in other content since then.

The Birkin has also been featured in television and movies, increasing its notoriety. When there was an episode of *Sex and the City* centered around Samantha coveting a bag and trying to cut the five-year waitlist, it is reported that the interest in the list increased by more than 300 percent.

Another feature of the Birkin is that it isn't covered in logos and doesn't have the Hermès name all over it; you often can't even see the brand name. And yet, everyone knows it's a Birkin. With its unique rectangular silhouette, elegant handles, and signature lock, the iconic shape of the Birkin is synonymous with Hermès and luxury. Their choice to be so understated makes it so people feel like they are part of the in-crowd just by knowing what it is. This allows the masses to be part of the exclusivity even when they can't purchase one themselves.

RECIPROCITY

One of my favorite aspects of the current version of the Birkin is that you need to be chosen by a sales associate to have the right to purchase a bag. Jerks need not apply. I love that this exclusivity is not just about how rich you are or how much status you have (though, obviously, that is a factor in being able to buy a bag), and it isn't about one-time purchases. You need to invest enough in the full Hermès brand to earn the right to a retail Birkin.

What is even more fantastic about this reciprocity model is that they aren't giving them away for free as a gift with many purchases—this gift is the right to purchase your bag at retail for tens of thousands of dollars. We of course don't know for sure that they have never given a bag away for free, but that is definitely not the model, and I love that lesson for brands.

LOSS AVERSION

When someone is given a chance to buy their Birkin, they take it. Not the right size? Get smaller stuff to fit in the bag you were offered. Not your favorite color? Learn to love it and style a wardrobe around it. If and when your name wins the Birkin lottery, you say thank you (or more likely, squeal with delight) and pay a million pretty pennies for your coveted new treasure.

Because of the extreme scarcity, the resale market also touts how patrons looking for a specific Birkin color or design need to be ready to pounce and purchase whenever their desired bag surfaces. You might have to wait years for the bag you are looking for to come available, so people know if you see one you like and you are in the market for it, buy it. And, because Birkins have always gone up in value, in the worst case, people rationalize them as a great investment so it is worth the risk.

PRIMING

The prestige of the Birkin—and by association, the entire Hermès brand—precedes it. People don't just talk about it being "leather"; it is the most supple leather you've ever felt. That rare one that sold for half a million? It is the thirty-centimeter diamond Himalayan Birkin. Remember, adjectives are your friend when it comes to priming, and the Birkin has those in spades. An article in *Vogue* described it by saying, "the bag is made of Nilo crocodile, rendered in a subtle coloration that is meant to evoke images of the majestic Himalayan mountains. This dyeing process is painstaking and takes many hours to complete... The color pairs perfectly with eighteen-karat white gold hardware, which is itself studded with white diamonds."[104]

Hermès as a larger brand is no stranger to priming. Even their signature orange boxes and shopping bags are a way people can know someone was shopping at the iconic brand without even seeing the name or logo.

FRAMING

Much like the description from Serendipity3, Hermès and the Birkin are positioned as the ultimate luxury—a coveted heirloom that only the crème de la crème are given the opportunity to buy. It's not just a bag. It's a Birkin.

Everything about it is framed as an experience unto itself. This is a brand that owns its quality—both in the way it is produced and its limited supply.

One last interesting thing I want to mention about Hermès is that they started as a harness workshop in 1837. They got their origins making saddles, bridles, and other leather riding gear for noblemen and didn't start making bags until 1922. Because this section was about the Birkin bag specifically, we didn't even talk about what Hermès is perhaps best known for: scarves. This is a massive departure from leather and metal, and the brand didn't open their first scarf factory until 1937.[105] While Hermès has been producing these luxury items for decades, the company's ability to adapt and expand into new areas such as scarves shows how strategic changes can add value to an already successful business. Expansion and change—made possible with mental reframes—are an important part of any business, and one that is exemplified by Hermès.

VALUE + SERVICE: RYANAIR

Ryanair's reputation as Europe's leading low-cost airline isn't a coincidence; it's a carefully crafted image that relies on strategies like priming, social proof, reciprocity, and more. Here's how they do it. The company, which began its operations in 1984, relaunched itself as "Europe's first low fares airline" in 1990. The airline has cut costs and frills in the decades that followed, streamlining everything in the name of low fares.

PRIMING

On a recent trip to London, I was given an opportunity to visit a friend in Belfast. Never having been to Ireland, I was excited at the prospect, but of course (knowing how expensive travel can be) I was worried the cost of the trip might be prohibitive. Being from the states, I had heard the name Ryanair and knew they were synonymous with cheap travel, so that was where my search began. Flights on Ryanair were £17 each way (about $35 roundtrip) from London to Belfast. It was an easy purchase; the car I took to the London Stansted airport was considerably more than the flights.

The brand's reputation precedes it—there was no question who to look to when I wanted an inexpensive flight. This is because of the priming that comes from a brand that knows what it is about: cheap flights. While they streamline everything in favor of affordability, Ryanair adheres to standard airline safety regulations, ensuring that passengers can trust in their safety just as they would with a more expensive carrier. They don't waste money on fancy advertisements or unnecessary amenities, but instead keep it simple to save passengers even more money. Their brand is all about value, and you feel it in every interaction.

SOCIAL PROOF

Ryanair has made many headlines over the years (and been the source of a joke or two) for their no-frills, cheap travel. Their CEO once made a controversial remark about charging passengers for using the bathroom. Though shocking to some, it is consistent with Ryanair's brand. It underscores their commitment to cutting costs and emphasizes that they're willing to take unconventional approaches to keep fares low.[106]

While some of the authors of those articles and social posts were likely outraged at the audacity of an airline suggesting such a thing...think about what perfect press this was for Ryanair!

For their target market—people looking for the cheapest possible travel options—do you think there is any question whether or not Ryanair is doing everything they can to cut costs? Stories like these stick in your mind and you believe them to be true because they are "earned media," rather than something the company paid for (which also helps to show they aren't spending money on PR). If this was a planned PR stunt by the company, I say, "Bravo."

The other type of social proof you get from Ryanair is recommendations from friends and family members. As I have talked about my trip to Belfast, you can be sure I bragged about how inexpensive the flight was. And, while there were no luxuries, I was jealous of everyone living in Europe that has this option, allowing them to travel to wonderful locations more often. With three kids, it isn't cheap for my husband and I to take the family on trips, and we would absolutely take advantage of Ryanair if we lived nearby.

RECIPROCITY

Reciprocity here refers to Ryanair's practice of providing only what the customer pays for, without hidden charges for services they might not use. This ensures that the customer receives exactly what they value, creating a sense of fair exchange. It is true that to some, it may not seem like their no-frills approach is a "gift"—to the wrong clientele it may feel like they are just cheap for no reason. But for their target market, they are a dream! Even if you don't care about reclining seats and don't eat the snacks provided on another airline, you still have to pay for them. Don't use the pocket to store your belongings? You still pay for it to be there and to be cleaned between flights (which costs the airline money to maintain, a cost that is passed along to their customers). While you can't pay for a seat that reclines or a pocket on the seat in front of you even if you wanted to on Ryanair, since these aren't even options, you know you aren't being charged for it. And you don't have to pay for other people to have water or to put ice on the plane. If you want it, you pay for it. If you don't, you can keep that cheapest possible flight. Win!

This is a gift to those who wouldn't be able to travel otherwise and something that I'm sure Ryanair's target market appreciates. Ryanair also now offers cars for hire, hotels, and experiences which can be booked on their website, which is a smart extension of the core brand. Because they are known for being a great deal, that brand promise extends to everything you buy from them. There is no need to look around because you know they are getting you the best deal possible.

True, they aren't for everyone, and that is the whole point. There is no question about what you get when you choose Ryanair. If it isn't for you, there are other options, and people can easily self-select their best choice without having to talk to an agent (which would cost money) because they are so clear and transparent in their messaging.

ANCHORING

Ryanair has the benefit of standard airline pricing as their high anchor. A quick search on Expedia right now brought back roundtrip tickets from London to Belfast for $108, $121, and $148 among others. Compare that with the $35 I paid on Ryanair, and there is a clear difference. (To be fair, those flights are still far less than what I pay to fly from Seattle to Portland or Los Angeles, so even those high anchors are still a pretty great deal to me, but for those who are used to seeing outrageous prices for flights, there is a clear high anchor that makes the low fares from Ryanair a delightful surprise.)

LOSS AVERSION AND SCARCITY

Ryanair leverages both loss aversion and scarcity to drive sales. By highlighting limited seat availability and exclusive low prices, they create a sense of urgency, encouraging customers to book quickly to avoid missing out on deals. Airline pricing is still going to vary based on when you buy, so you know there are a limited number of seats available on the plane and at any given price. Like any airline, they have time-based scarcity and demand scarcity going for them—more people talking about them means there are less seats available for you, so you'd better act fast!

FRAMING

Ryanair's intentionally simple and somewhat outdated website design is not a flaw but a strategy. By avoiding flashy updates, they reinforce their no-frills, cost-saving image, making it clear to customers that every penny saved is passed on to them in the form of low fares. Again, this just reinforces the message that Ryanair is providing great value for their customers without wasting money on anything unnecessary.

In addition, Ryanair's deliberate choice of the word "cheap" over "inexpensive" on their website and in Google searches is more than semantics; it's a bold statement that aligns with their core value proposition. By embracing a term that many might shy away from, they cement their image as a no-nonsense, budget-friendly option for the savvy traveler. That word is definitely not chosen by accident. It conveys something different about them than the reframe most would choose of "inexpensive" does. They're cheap and they know it—and so does everyone else.

VALUE + PRODUCT:
OLD NAVY

Old Navy is a value-focused fashion brand that first launched in 1994 and now has over 1,200 locations around the world. As the fastest retailer to reach $1 billion in sales within four years, Old Navy's unique approach to affordable fashion clearly struck a chord with consumers. With bright colors and fun advertising, they have always had a relatable vibe. On the history page of their website, they call their launch a "revolution" and that they "were something the world had never seen— fabulous, affordable fashion for everyone."[107]

SOCIAL PROOF

When I think of Old Navy, in addition to bright colors and a dog mannequin in every store, I also think of all the celebrities who have been in its humorous ads: Amy Pohler, Julia Louis Dreyfus, Lil Kim, Amy Schumer, Neil Patrick Harris, Jennifer Coolidge, Morgan Fairchild...the list goes on. Even though the celebrities are paid to be featured in these ads (and may not wear Old Navy items outside of the time they are paid to do so during filming), this social proof carries great weight in the value people see in the ad. We know they are paid to wear those holiday pajama sets or dance around in the performance fleece...but it also feels like they *chose* to rep the brand, so we should too. Old Navy is also affordable, making it easy for people to get lots of great looks at a great price. That means more people wear it more often, reinforcing the social proof aspect of the brand.

SCARCITY

Old Navy has mastered sales. In addition to their everyday low prices, they have regular sales that are tied to moments—like back to school—when they know their ideal customers need to buy a lot of clothes and are looking for a deal. Kids need new shorts? Old Navy. Fun flip flops? Old Navy. Suzy's baby shower? Old Navy.

On a visit to their website during the writing of this book, five coupons popped up. Two of them say "Today only!" in bright red font—they are for 50 percent off adult button-downs and 50 percent off kids' uniforms. There is also an online clearance coupon (with no code required) saying there is 25 percent off the whole site (which ends today). "This week only" kids' backpacks are just $18. The last promotion showcases the fact that Navyist credit card users get 30 percent off their order. Wow, that's a lot of deals.

One thing I've always admired about Old Navy is how they use delayed rewards to get you to come back. It is common when making a purchase there to either receive a coupon or note on the receipt or get an email from them saying you earned a discount or Super Cash to use on a future purchase. The genius here is that they are only eligible to be used during a specific date range. So, let's say a customer bought back to school clothes for the kids in August. At that time, they might get a promotion saying they have earned $10 off every $25 spent if they come back September 5–15. The great value makes them start to imagine what they could buy (triggering loss aversion). And Old Navy knows they will be doing other sales (and seeing massive shopper traffic) Labor Day weekend before kids go back to school. They aren't encouraging these customers to come back then (because they likely would do that anyway—and still might). The promotion is instead for just *after* that time. This helps stabilize their sales pipeline and can **nudge** someone to shop when they might not have made a trip to the store, which is a huge win for Old Navy, which knows their customers don't just buy one or two things, they tend to buy a bunch. For them, extra visits are a huge win, and these short-term promotions are catered to encourage that.

LOSS AVERSION

As mentioned in the last section, rewards promotions that are earned on one trip to encourage another trip in the near future are a super smart way to trigger loss aversion. If someone knows they can get $10 off when they spend $25 in just a couple of weeks, their mind starts imagining everything they could get to redeem that value.

If customers found something they really liked but chose not to purchase on the day, they might be enticed to return and buy it later. Or perhaps they will start looking around their closet to see what gap they might need to fill on that next trip. The important thing for you to see in this type of promotion is that it makes it more tangible and real than a more generic sale.

The timeliness of the coupon—as you paid for your items—is key to this. You know the customer was just in the store and likely tried a lot of stuff on. Old Navy has so many options for everyone in the family, it is also very likely that the customer saw at least a few things they chose not to buy today. A great deal that is far enough away (but not too far) will let someone plan and budget to come back *next month* to take advantage of (and not miss out on) that deal they earned. If your value and product-based business is interested in increasing trips to your store (which most such businesses probably are), whether you are brick-and-mortar or virtual, you can learn a lot of great tips from Old Navy's strategy.

RECIPROCITY

While Ryanair is all about "cheap" and that is a gift to their customers, Old Navy is giving a different type of gift: stylish clothes at a great price. Without Old Navy, if you are on a budget, you may feel like you or your kids will be limited to plain items that stand out in a way they don't want (especially at school, where other kids aren't always kind). Old Navy has licensing deals with tons of iconic brands: Hello Kitty, Marvel, Batman, Star Wars, Mario, ET, Sonic the Hedgehog, and Pokémon, to name a few.[108]

While other companies may sell licensed shirts like these for $40–$75 or more, you can get them from Old Navy for $14.99—and that's before they go on sale. Given how quickly kids outgrow clothes (and trends), it is a huge gift to their clientele to offer on-trend items at a great price.

This convenient and enjoyable shopping experience, where every family member can find something they like, feels like a gift to many customers, particularly parents. Every member of the family can be picking out items in one store (and for every parent who has had one kid complaining and asking "When will it be *my* turn? This is so *boring!*" you know what a gift this is).

Another fantastic thing about Old Navy is their dedication to a more diverse audience. In 2021, they launched *Bodequality*, which means they carry all women's styles in size 0–30 with no price difference. In case you didn't know, most brands charge more money for larger sizes than they do for smaller sizes. The rationale is that it takes more fabric to make larger pieces, but this can of course feel unfair for those who have to pay more for the same items. As *Business Insider* reported (a couple of years before the launch of Bodequality), a straight size shirt (XS-XXL) at Old Navy cost $16.99 and a plus size of the same shirt was $19.99.[109] What I love about this example is that Old Navy clearly heard their customers, knew what mattered to them and what aligned with the company's mission of "fabulous affordable fashion for everyone," and realized they needed to make a change. That is a true gift to their customers (and something that garnered them positive social proof, resulting in a win-win).

PRIMING AND FRAMING

Old Navy excels at embodying their brand values in every aspect of their business, from advertising and in-store experience to product quality and pricing. They are about value, and you see that everywhere when you interact with their brand. (If you walk by a store, there is always a big banner for some sale or another, their website is full of coupons and short-term sales, and their advertisements are promoting their fun fashions and great deals for the whole family.) This is a great example of being able to provide quality items at a great value; they aren't made to last for generations, but they don't fall apart either.

The bright, bold colors and fun fonts on their ads draw you in and make you want to engage with them. The store is bright and cheerful. Even though there are a *lot* of items in there, it doesn't feel cluttered. The space is well organized, and it's easy to find what you are looking for. The checkout has tons of trinkets and add-ons to keep people engaged (and tossing those last items into a shopping basket) while they are waiting in line.

Old Navy is a great value, and you feel it in every interaction with the brand.

CHAPTER 14

IF YOU'RE IN A RUSH

As promised, this chapter is for all the people who have realized that for whatever reason, they need to set a price in a very, very short time (less than a week) and don't have the time to dedicate to going through the full process outlined in this book before that time.

At these moments of **time pressure**, your brain would otherwise lead you to stress and **bikeshed** (i.e., productively procrastinate) so long that you end up with the last resort: relying on a common tendency to follow what others are doing (resorting to those natural **herding** instincts) and picking a price that is close to the competition or otherwise feels safe.

Hopefully you know this without me saying it, but just in case, the process outlined in this chapter won't be as impactful as doing everything in the book (if that were the case, I wouldn't have taken the time to include all the other stuff for you). This chapter and its tasks will give you enough insight to help you feel confident in picking a price that will get you through this moment so you can have a better experience than if you didn't include any behavioral insights into the process.

TASK: READ THESE CHAPTERS

While time may be limited, understanding why behavioral economics is important to your buying process can provide you with valuable insights. It's well worth a brief exploration before you start to apply anything. These two chapters will give you some insight into your own brain so you won't get stuck and can move through this process to confidently choose your prices.

- Chapter 3: Pricing, Placement, and Psychology

- Chapter 4: You

TASK: ANSWER THESE QUESTIONS

- The Customer and the Offer

  - Who is this for?

  - What are you selling?

  - What problem does this solve for them?

  - What is the value of solving that problem for them?

  - What do you want them to do?

  - What are they doing now (instead of what you think they should)?

  - Where will you be communicating this message?

  - What will be going on in their mind/life when they see this?

  - If someone will only do one thing after seeing this, what is that most important thing?

  - What is going to compel them to stop what they are doing and take another action?

  - Where will they get stuck?

  - What happens if they do nothing?

  - What is the least you can say to get them to buy?

- The Market and the Company

  - Who is your main competitor?

  - What type of company are they? (Quality or Value)

  - What is their pricing model?

  - What type of company are you? (Quality or Value)

  - How is their messaging different than yours?

  - How do your models differ? What is the benefit of choosing you?

  - If your customers could only know one thing about you, what would you want it to be?

- The Numbers

  - What is your break-even point on this item?

  - How much do you want to make from this over the year?

  - What is your goal with this immediate launch/promo that has you in a rush (in terms of dollars and units sold)?

  - Ideally, what would you charge for this?

TASK: READ THESE CHAPTERS

Now that you have answered those questions, you have a foundation to jump into application. These chapters each have tasks, which you should do before executing any pricing and placement strategy.

- Chapter 10: The Framework

  - If you have time and are looking for some inspiration for how this is used in other companies, check out Chapter 13: Examples as well. One of the four case studies will be the closest fit to your type of business, depending on whether you are quality or value, product- or service-based.

- Chapter 11: The Choice
- Chapter 12: The Placement

The tasks outlined in those three chapters will give you what you need to select a price as well as how to present it to your customer. They include templates to help you create charts, descriptions for when you have vertically stacked explanations (as is often the case on a website product page and in email pitches), and scripts for your sales staff. Each of these can be customized to help you feel confident in your new pricing strategy so you can have success pitching right away.

TASK: MAKE TIME ON YOUR CALENDAR

Now we both know (since you have read Chapter 3: Pricing, Placement, and Psychology) that **time discounting** and **optimism bias** will make you think you will remember to come back and revisit the full process later on—but somehow other things will always get in the way. You picked up this book because you want to have a brainy pricing strategy. You want to make it so it is easy for your perfect customers to naturally choose you. You want people to buy (and be excited) without you having to sell them constantly.

That is possible if you go through and complete the full process outlined in this book. The foundation matters, and your dedication to understanding and applying these principles can make a tangible difference in your success. So, while this "In a Rush" process will get you through your immediate launch, it isn't going to do all of what you, your company, and your customers deserve.

Take a minute now to look at your calendar. Find a thirty-day span within the next six months where you will read the full book and complete the other tasks within it. Consider the time of day and an approach that works best for your style. That might be a set time per day where you make it a ritual with your morning coffee.

It could require steps where you integrate larger teams into the discussion and process. Think it through, mark it on your calendar, set a reminder, and get an accountability buddy. Explain to this person what you are doing and when you want them to check in with you to keep you on track.

And with that...happy pricing!

FROM THIS CHAPTER

Tasks:

- Read Chapters 3 and 4.
- Answer these questions.
- Read Chapters 10, 11, and 12.
- Make time on your calendar.

Key Terms:

- Time Pressure
- Bikeshedding
- Herding
- Time Discounting
- Optimism Bias

CHAPTER 15

BACK TO YOU

Wow. How are you feeling? Now that you've come this far, do you feel a sense of accomplishment and readiness, or perhaps a touch of hesitation? Maybe a bit of both? Wherever you land on that scale, know that it is normal to feel a mix of emotions right now as your brain is realizing change is near. Whether it is because you have a different model than the rest of your industry or are looking to raise your prices for the first time or anything else, it is natural to feel a little anticipation as you prepare to go live with your new brainy pricing. Remember, your brain is wired to be scared of the unknown. It wants to keep you in the status quo. This final chapter is an opportunity to explore what comes next and get your new brainy pricing strategy over the finish line.

TASK: PRACTICE SAYING IT

For the customer to feel comfortable saying yes, confidently stating your price is key. (Note: This applies to everyone who will talk about the price or sell on your behalf.) When people hedge and skirt around the pricing or are hesitant...the customer can sense something is off. It pushes people away and will keep them from buying. You didn't put in all this work to stop five feet from the finish line!

What you need to do now is to be able to say your price as if you are saying the time of day or the weather. It needs to be easy. It needs to become your brain's new status quo. When someone asks, "How much is it?" you need to have your new default response ready to go without much conscious thought.

This will take practice. This is especially true if you have had your old pricing for a long time or are significantly increasing your rates. And it isn't enough to *think* it. You need to say it aloud—multiple times. You have to really believe it!

Early in my career, I was working at an advertising agency which had selected my hourly rate for me. I don't remember exactly what it was, but it was definitely more than I would have been able to afford as a recent college graduate. It was a small agency, so the woman who worked in reception was also the accountant. She was this wonderful grandmotherly type named Liz. I used to love to sit and chat with her for a few minutes each day. I'm not sure what triggered her to say it, but one day she said to me, "Remember this, Melina: You are worth every penny of your hourly rate. Don't ever feel bad about charging what you are worth."

Those words have stuck with me through the years, and I want you to feel them too. Whatever the number, be it ten or ten million, you are worth it. Never feel bad about charging what you are worth.

I'd like to share one more helpful tip from my early career. What feels like a lifetime ago, I worked in the call center for an airline. (Sidenote: Always be kind to the person on the phone or at the desk trying to help you. They're humans trying to do a job and often didn't cause whatever issue you're both trying to resolve.) At the airline, they taught us to say every price with a smile—no matter how outrageous you thought it was—present a call to action, and then wait for the customer's response.

There were a couple of key lessons here. First, you don't know what that person on the phone values. For me as an eighteen-year-old, money was a huge motivator. I would happily fly out an hour earlier or later to save a hundred dollars. For a business traveler needing to make an important meeting, they might not care as much about saving money. It wasn't my job to layer the offer with my personal motivations because they weren't relevant to that buyer's decision.

My job was to say the price as it came up: "That flight from Seattle to Dallas will be $4,378.52. Would you like to purchase that today?" I said it with a smile and would wait for as long as it took for them to respond. Sometimes, as shocking as it was to me then, they would say, "Yup, let's do it." Going through this experience multiple times was a big learning experience for me in what people value.

If they said instead, "Whoa! That's crazy. Do you have anything cheaper?" I could ask some follow-up questions about how flexible they were on the day, time, number of connections, and anything else to help find an option that fit their needs.

When the Price Is the Price

There are some people who are conditioned to always ask for a discount. This doesn't mean you have to offer them one—or that they won't pay full price if you say no. Pricing integrity matters, so don't be afraid to hold firm on your price. Think back to the type of brand you are. Not everyone is your customer. If you provide a high-end experience, you will be too expensive for many people. That is okay. Know what you are about and why you chose the prices you have. If you have decided not to offer discounts, own it. Always be kind, and also know that you don't have to apologize or explain yourself.

The second big thing I learned in my time at the airline was to always have that call to action. If I just said the price and sat there waiting for the other person to respond, it would have been super weird! I had to say, "Would you like to move forward with purchasing that today?" to let them know that now was the time to make a decision.

You would be shocked by how often I am brought in to help a company with their pricing and sales only to find out that they don't have a clear call to action. Their staff never asks, and there is no button or link on any electronic communications. Don't make it hard for people to buy from you!

Every page on your website needs at least one call to action, but be careful not to overload with too many. This is why understanding the journey is so important. The call to action on one page might be to get your lead magnet or sign up for your newsletter. Another page might be to book a call. Another might be to buy something. Make it simple and help people to know the next small step in their process.

Smart calls to action help leverage **herding** instincts, the phenomenon where people follow the crowd's behavior. By essentially saying, "Most people are ready to buy now—are you?" you are tapping into this instinct. For anyone who isn't, make it easy to learn more or take a follow-up action. For example, have a small text link that says "Learn More" underneath a prominent "Buy Now" button so anyone who isn't quite ready to buy but is still interested can get more information instead of ending their journey there. (Make sure that small "Learn More" link isn't the only option and don't make it so big that it makes anyone who was ready to buy question if they need to do more research first.) If you don't make it easy to buy, people will leave. And that isn't good for either of you.

TASK: TAKE A TIP FROM NIKE

Another question I am often asked is, "How can I get comfortable with my new pricing?" Well, like it or not, at some point you have to jump in and start using it. Or borrowing from Nike:

"Just Do It."

You can't get comfortable with it until you live it. Even if it is scary, do whatever you need to do to bolster your confidence and try it. I have found success listening to a power song that helps me feel centered before going into a big sales call (yes, even I get anxious when quoting prices). Others like to meditate, chat with someone who will remind them how awesome they are, or do a role-play where they get to practice that big pitch one or two more times.

Whatever you need to do, do it. And even if you're scared—just do it.

Remember that the pricing you are quoting now isn't forever. Everything is an opportunity to test. Commit to this new pricing for thirty days (or however long you need to have a reasonable amount of feedback). But you must believe it and say it confidently, or it doesn't count. Even if you feel worried about what might happen if you fail, **reframe** your status quo-loving brain. Give yourself a goal—what would get you motivated to push through and try this thing?

Imagine rewarding yourself with a vacation if you hit your sales goal, or a new computer, or even hiring a new employee. What's your motivation?

To keep you motivated, **prime** yourself with a visual of that goal—display it prominently in your selling space. (Use the details in the next section to come share it with me on social media, I can't wait to see it!) When you own this pricing and go all in on it, you will be amazed at how easy selling (and closing!) becomes.

Trust me, I've seen success with this approach again and again. I want that success for you too.

TASK: CONNECT, SHARE, AND GET YOUR FREEBIES

I hope you have gotten immense value from the insights in this book and that you are ready to move forward confidently with your brainy pricing strategy. Now that you've made it to the end of the book (congratulations!), I would love to hear from you—your thoughts, your wins, your questions—so please take a moment to connect and share on social media. And, of course, if you haven't gotten your freebies yet, be sure to visit the website to get those. Tag and follow **@thebrainybiz** on social media and Melina Palmer on LinkedIn.

- Follow **#TruthAboutPricing** to connect and see insights from others (and use the hashtag yourself to share insights, success stories, and anything else that has you inspired!)

- When you have a question, use **#PricingQuestion** (and follow this hashtag too if you want to see how I answer other reader questions)

- Get all your freebies, including the Pricing Mastery Checklist and virtual glossary using this QR code and at *thebrainybusiness.com/pricing-book*.

Get your free Pricing Mastery Checklist and glossary with the QR code and at thebrainybusiness.com/pricing-book

Congratulations in advance for all your brainy pricing success. And as always, remember to BE thoughtful.

—Melina

FROM THIS CHAPTER

Tasks:

- Practice saying it.
- Take a tip from Nike.
- Connect, share, and get your freebies.

Key Terms:

- Framing
- Herding
- Nudge
- Status Quo Bias
- Priming

AFTERWORD

I hope you've enjoyed all the insights, tips, and stories throughout *The Truth About Pricing*. And, because you now know the value of asking for things, giving generously, and social proof...I have a request:

- Will you rate and review this book on Amazon, GoodReads, Google, or any other platform?
- If you can think of one person who would enjoy the book, will you recommend it to them?
- If something resonated with you while reading—maybe you highlighted as you read, like I do—will you share it on social media and tag me @thebrainybiz #TruthAboutPricing so I can connect with you?

Celebrating with listeners of *The Brainy Business* podcast and fans of my books who have implemented their learnings and seen success is one of my favorite things. I will always love to hear from you. Got a question? Come ask me! I love chatting about behavioral economics and can't wait to have a great conversation with you.

For everyone who is looking for more brainy insights, please do visit *thebrainybusiness.com*—there are courses and lots of great content available for you there to continue your learning (including the freebies that accompany this book at *thebrainybusiness.com/pricing-book*). You can also subscribe to *The Brainy Business* podcast, with new episodes every week.

You can also learn about my other books, including the award-winning *What Your Customer Wants and Can't Tell You* and *What Your Employees Need and Can't Tell You*. More about any of my books can be found at *thebrainybusiness.com/books*.

Want to work together? The Brainy Business provides consulting for all types and sizes of businesses, from solopreneurs to global corporations. I can't wait to hear from and work with you! Visit *thebrainybusiness.com* to learn more and get started.

And of course, if you are looking for a speaker on pricing and/or using behavioral economics to help customers buy and employees to buy in, email *melina@thebrainybusiness.com*.

Thank you again for reading *The Truth About Pricing*. I hope you found great value within its pages and that you start to reap the brainy rewards right away!

BE thoughtful,

—*Melina*

ACKNOWLEDGEMENTS

This book would not have been possible without the support and kindness of so many people and organizations. Thank you all for everything you have done to make this possible.

First and foremost, to my husband Aaron. Thank you for your patience, for your support—for hours spent reading, providing feedback, talking through ideas, and being my rock. This could not have happened without you. And, of course, thank you to the rest of the family for your patience and understanding during the many late nights, missed meals, and hours spent locked away with noise-canceling headphones on.

To Kwame Christian, thank you for your friendship, kindness, and support over the years. I always appreciate and value your thoughts and advice. And of course, thank you for being my forewordist—I am honored you agreed to support me in this way.

To MJ Fievre, thank you for all your thoughtful edits, feedback, and words of encouragement. You made this book better than I could have on my own. I am so grateful for you and the entire Mango team. Thank you for believing in me and helping all three of my books to come to fruition!

And to everyone else who has helped shape *The Brainy Business* podcast and this book, *The Truth About Pricing*, by providing interviews, stories, time, support, sharing, listening, and so much more during the writing process and beyond: Thank you. There is not room here to list all the names, but I want to thank everyone quoted or otherwise represented in this book once more, as well as a few amazing people who have always been there for me. In alphabetical order, thank you: Amy Bucher, Ayelet Fishbach, Brian Ahearn,

Chris Rawlinson, Christian Hunt, Dan Gingiss, Dilip Soman, David McRaney, Gleb Tsipursky, Jeff Pool, Jennifer Clinehens, Jez Groom, Jo Evershed, John List, Jonah Berger, Katelyn Bourgoin, Louise Brogan, Marco Palma, Marcus Collins, Matt Johnson, Michael Hallsworth, Michael Schein, Mindy Weinstein, Nancy Harhut, Nikki Rausch, Nir Eyal, Nuala Walsh, Richard Chataway, Richard Shotton, Robert Cialdini, Roger Dooley, Sam Evans, Scott Miller, Stephen Wendel, Tessa Misiaszek, Vanessa Bohns, Will Leach, Zoe Chance.

Last, but not least, thank you to all the listeners, subscribers, sharers, and supporters of *The Brainy Business* podcast. Without you, none of this would be here. Thank you.

ABOUT THE AUTHOR

Melina Palmer is on a mission to help businesses be more brain friendly, with a focus on applying behavioral economics to help customers buy and employees buy in. A globally celebrated keynote speaker, Melina has been honored to present for SXSW, Walmart, Maker's Mark, the American Marketing Association, and for many other conferences, corporations, and small businesses.

She is CEO of The Brainy Business, which provides behavioral economics training and consulting to businesses of all sizes from around the world. Her podcast, *The Brainy Business: Understanding the Psychology of Why People Buy*, has more than a million downloads from over 170 countries and is used as a resource for teaching applied behavioral economics for many universities and businesses. Melina teaches applied behavioral economics through the Texas A&M Human Behavior Lab and obtained her master's in behavioral economics from The Chicago School of Professional Psychology. A proud member of the Global Association of Applied Behavioral Scientists, Melina has contributed research to the Association for Consumer Research and the Filene Research Institute, and writes a Behavioral Economics & Business column for *Inc. Magazine*. She and her work have also been featured in *Psychology Today*, *Inc.*, *Business Insider*, *Business News Daily*, and more.

Her first book, *What Your Customer Wants and Can't Tell You*, was a finalist in two categories of the International Book Awards and won first place in the Chanticleer International Book Awards. Her second book, *What Your Employees Need and Can't Tell You*, was a finalist in the Chanticleer International Book Awards.

@thebrainybiz: Twitter (X), Instagram, Threads, Facebook
/thebrainybusiness: YouTube
Melina Palmer: LinkedIn

ENDNOTES

1   Kahneman, D. (2011). *Thinking, fast and slow.* Farrar, Straus and Giroux.

2   Pradeep, A.K. (2010). *The buying brain: Secrets for selling to the subconscious mind.* John Wiley & Sons.

3   Graff, F. (2018, February 7). How many daily decisions do we make? *Science.* Retrieved from: science.unctv.org/content/reportersblog/choices.

4   Zaltman, G. (2003). *How customers think.* Harvard Business School Press.

5   Palmer, M. (Host). (2020, November 20). Good habits, bad habits: An interview with Wendy Wood (No. 127) [Audio podcast episode]. In *The Brainy Business.*

6   Morse, G. (2002, June). Hidden minds. *Harvard Business Review.* Retrieved from: hbr. org/2002/06/hidden-minds; Walesh, S.G. (n.d.). Using the power of habits to work smarter. *Helping You Engineer Your Future blog.* Retrieved from: www.helpingyouengineeryourfuture. com/habits-work-smarter.htm.

7   Ash, T. (2021). *Unleash your primal brain: Demystifying how we think and why we act.* Morgan James Publishing.

8   Staff. (n.d.) Is sheldon right about staircases? Will a 2mm difference in one step cause people to trip? *Levin & Malkin blog.* Retrieved from: levinandmalkin.com/is-sheldon-right-about-staircases-will-a-2mm-difference-in-one-step-cause-people-to-trip.

9   Metcalfe, J. (2012, July 2). New York City fixes mayhem-causing subway stair. *Bloomberg.* Retrieved from: www.bloomberg.com/news/articles/2012-07-02/new-york-city-fixes-mayhem-causing-subway-stair.

10   Palmer, M. (Host). (2022, August 18). Do nudges work? With Michael Hallsworth (No. 218) [Audio podcast episode]. In *The Brainy Business.*

11   Schwartz, B. (2004). *The paradox of choice: Why more is less.* HarperCollins; Palmer, M. (Host). (2021, September 24). Paradox of choice (No. 171) [Audio podcast episode]. In *The Brainy Business.*

12   Krissilas, J. (2010, May 19). Weighing our options. *Planning Notepad.* Retrieved from: www. planningnotepad.com/2010/03/weighing-our-options.html; Karten, N. (2012, September 20). How you can overcome the paradox of choice. *Techwell.* Retrieved from: www.techwell.com/ techwell-insights/2012/09/how-you-can-overcome-paradox-choice; Staff. (n.d.). Paradox of choice. *Model Thinkers.* Retrieved from: modelthinkers.com/mental-model/paradox-of-choice.

13   Cialdini, R. B. (2021). *Influence, new and expanded: The psychology of persuasion.* Harper Business.

14   Sharot, T. (2012, February). *The optimism bias* [Video]. TED Conferences. www.ted.com/ talks/tali_sharot_the_optimism_bias; Palmer, M. (Host). (2019, February 8). Optimism bias: The good and the bad of those rose-colored glasses (No. 34) [Audio podcast episode]. In *The Brainy Business.*

15   Kahneman, D., & Tversky, A. (1979). Intuitive prediction: Biases and corrective procedures. *Management Science, 12,* 313–327.

16   Kahneman, D. (2011). *Thinking, fast and slow.* Farrar, Straus and Giroux. (pp 325–326); Palmer, M. (Host). (2020, August 21). Stressed and overcommitted? Tips to tackle planning fallacy (No. 114) [Audio podcast episode]. In *The Brainy Business*.

17   Buehler, R., Griffin, D., & Ross, M. (1994). Exploring the "planning fallacy": Why people underestimate their task completion times. *Journal of Personality and Social Psychology, 679(3)*, 366–381.

18   Dragicevic, P. & Jansen, Y. (2014). Visualization-mediated alleviation of the planning fallacy. *DECISIVe: Workshop on Dealing with Cognitive Biases in Visualizations.* Retrieved from: hal.inria.fr/hal-01500560/document.

19   Hershfield, H. (2023). *Your future self: How to make tomorrow better today.* Little, Brown Spark.; Palmer, M. (Host). (2023, October 6). Your future self, with Hal Hershfield (No. 329) [Audio podcast episode]. In *The Brainy Business*.

20   Palmer, M. (Host). (2020, May 8). Bikeshedding: Why the simplest tasks can keep you stuck (No. 99) [Audio podcast episode]. In *The Brainy Business*.; Wigmore, I. (April 2015). Parkinson's law of triviality (bikeshedding). *WhatIs.com.* Retrieved from: whatis. techtarget.com/definition/Parkinsons-law-of-triviality-bikeshedding.

21   Terao, Y., Fukuda, H., & Hikosaka, O. (2017). What do eye movements tell us about patients with neurological disorders?—An introduction to saccade recording in the clinical setting. Proceedings of the Japan Academy. *Series B, Physical and Biological Sciences, 93*(10), 772–801.

22   *Küpfer*, S. (2023, February 8). Twenty-three minutes. *Get Abstract.* Retrieved from: journal.getabstract.com/en/2022/03/17/twenty-three-minutes.

23   CNNWire. (2021, July 28). Manhattan restaurant unveils $200 french fries, setting Guinness World Record. *ABC 7 NY.* Retrieved from: abc7ny.com/serendipity-3-most-expensive-french-fries-200-new-york-city/10915270; Martin, E. (2017, October 25). The most expensive grilled cheese in the world costs $214 and is gilded with real gold. *CNBC.* Retrieved from: www.cnbc.com/2017/10/25/most-expensive-grilled-cheese-in-the-world-from-serendipity-3.html.

24   Staff. (2004, November 17). 'Virgin Mary grilled cheese' sells for $28,000. *NBC News.* Retrieved from: www.nbcnews.com/id/wbna6511148.

25   Staff. (2018, January 23). 29 Rare supreme items that only hardcore collectors actually own. *Capital FM.* Retrieved from: www.capitalfm.com/features/weirdest-supreme-items; Takanashi, L. (2020, November 20). Hit or brick? Supreme's 10 weirdest items. *Complex.* Retrieved from: www.complex.com/style/supreme-10-weirdest-items.

26   Strong, J. (2022, January 5). The most expensive supreme items to ever exist. *Sole.* Retrieved from: thesolesupplier.co.uk/news/the-most-expensive-supreme-items-to-ever-exist; Lenton, J. (n.d.). Behind the hype: Why is everyone so crazy about Supreme? *Ape to Gentleman.* Retrieved from: www.apetogentleman.com/behind-the-hype-why-is-everyone-so-crazy-about-supreme; Staff. (n.d.). Case study: Supreme's unconventional email marketing strategy. *Send Check It.* Retrieved from: sendcheckit.com/blog/case-study-supreme-email-marketing-strategy; McKinnon, T. (2022, May 13). The brilliant strategy behind Supreme's success. *Indigo Digital.* Retrieved from: www.indigo9digital. com/blog/the-brilliant-strategy-behind-supremes-success; Staff. (2018, February 8). Case study: Supreme streetwear's insane success. *Grow Revenue.* Retrieved from: growrevenue.io/supreme-streetwear-success.

27   Vega, N. (2022, September 26). 'Lightning just struck me': Why Costco's CFO says the price of the $1.50 hot dog and soda combo is 'forever.' *CNBC.* Retrieved from: www.cnbc. com/2022/09/26/costco-cfo-says-hot-dog-and-soda-combo-price-is-forever.html.

28   Crockett, Z. (2022, October 8). The economics of Costco rotisserie chicken.
The Hustle. Retrieved from: thehustle.co/the-economics-of-costco-rotisserie-
chicken/#:~:text=But%20over%20the%20past%2020,they've%20stayed%20ever%20
since.

29   Pomranz, M. (2020, September 22). Why is Costco's hot dog combo still so cheap? A death
threat. *Food & Wine*. Retrieved from: www.foodandwine.com/news/why-costco-hot-dog-
still-dollar-fifty.

30   Leffler, S. (2023, February 17). 6 facts you need to know about Costco's rotisserie
chicken. *Real Simple*. Retrieved from: www.realsimple.com/costco-rotisserie-chicken-
facts-7111269.

31   Palmer, M. (Host). (2019, May 9). Costco: A behavioral economics analysis. (No. 47) [Audio
podcast episode]. In *The Brainy Business*.

32   Staff. (n.d.). Costco net income 2010–2023 | COST. *Macro Trends*. Retrieved from: www.
macrotrends.net/stocks/charts/COST/costco/net-income.

33   Kahneman, D. & Tversky, A. (1979). Prospect theory: An analysis of decision under risk.
Econometrica, 47, 263–291.

34   Palmer, M. (Host). (2023, May 16). Empathy, storytelling, and success: A conversation with
Michelle Auerbach (refreshed episode). (No. 288) [Audio podcast episode]. In *The Brainy
Business*.

35   Significant Objects. (n.d.). Retrieved from: significantobjects.com.

36   Dorst, D. (2009, August 25). Russian figure. *Significant Objects*. Retrieved from:
significantobjects.com/2009/08/25/russian-figure.

37   Park, E. (2009, August 7). Cow vase. *Significant Objects*. Retrieved from:
significantobjects.com/2009/08/07/cow-vase.

38   Palmer, M. (Host). (2021, November 12). The power of us, interview with Dominic Packer
(refreshed episode) (No. 304) [Audio podcast episode]. In *The Brainy Business*; Van Bavel,
J. J., & Packer, D. J. (2021). *The power of us: Harnessing our shared identities to improve
performance, increase cooperation, and promote social harmony*. Little, Brown Spark.

39   Thaler, R. H., & Sunstein, C. R. (2008). *Nudge: Improving decisions about health, wealth,
and happiness*. Penguin Books.

40   Palmer, M. (Host). (2022, August 21). Creating content people can't help but engage with,
featuring Katelyn Bourgoin (No. 201) [Audio podcast episode]. In *The Brainy Business*.

41   Palmer, M. (Host). (2018, July 6). Do lead magnets work (and do you need one)? (No. 3)
[Audio podcast episode]. In *The Brainy Business*; Palmer, M. (Host). (2020, June 4). How
to revisit and update your lead magnets (No. 103) [Audio podcast episode]. In *The Brainy
Business*.

42   Wood, W. (2019). *Good habits, bad habits: The science of making positive changes*.
Farrar, Straus and Giroux.

43   Bergland, C. (2012, November 29). The neurochemicals of happiness. *Psychology
Today*. Retrieved from: psychologytoday.com/us/blog/the-athletes-way/201211/the-
neurochemicals-happiness; Palmer, M. (Host). (2020, October 23). Get your D.O.S.E. of
brain chemicals (No. 123) [Audio podcast episode]. In *The Brainy Business*.

44   Zak, P. (2014, October 28). Why your brain loves good storytelling. *Harvard Business
Review*.

45 Palmer, M. (Host). (2021, December 30). How to create remarkable experiences, with Dan Gingiss (No. 185) [Audio podcast episode]. In *The Brainy Business*.

46 Milkman, K. (2021). *How to change: The science of getting from where you are to where you want to be*. Portfolio; Dai, H., Milkman, K. L., & Riis, J. (2014). The fresh start effect: Temporal landmarks motivate aspirational behavior. *Management Science*, *60*(10), 2563–2582; Dai, H., Milkman, K. L., & Riis, J. (2015). Put your imperfections behind you: Temporal landmarks spur goal initiation when they signal new beginnings. *Psychological Science*, *26*(12), 1927–1936; Beshears, J., Dai, H., Milkman, K. L., & Benartzi, S. (2021). Using fresh starts to nudge increased retirement savings. *Organizational Behavior and Human Decision Processes*, *167*, 72–87; Palmer, M. (Host). (2021, May 7). How to change, interview with Katy Milkman (No. 151) [Audio podcast episode]. In *The Brainy Business*.

47 Johnson, M., & Misiaszek, T. (2022). *Branding that means business: How to build enduring bonds between brands, consumers and markets*. Economist Books.; Palmer, M. (Host). (2022, October 27). Branding that means business, with Matt Johnson (No. 231) [Audio podcast episode]. In *The Brainy Business*.; Palmer, M. (Host). (2022, November 10). Great brands care about people, with Dr. Tessa Misiaszek (No. 235) [Audio podcast episode]. In *The Brainy Business*.

48 Van Bavel, J. J., & Packer, D. J. (2021). *The power of us: Harnessing our shared identities to improve performance, increase cooperation, and promote social harmony*. Little, Brown Spark.; Collins, M. (2023). *For the culture: The power behind what we buy, what we do, and who we want to be*. PublicAffairs.

49 Graves, K. (n.d.). How memories (or lack of) influence our relationships. *Communicating Psychological Science*. Retrieved from: communicatingpsychologicalscience.com/blog/ how-memories-or-lack-of-influence-our-relationships; Heath, C. (2017, August 8). Your memories make you who you are. *Psychology Today*. Retrieved from: psychologytoday. com/us/blog/psychoanalysis-unplugged/201708/your-memories-make-you-who-you-are.

50 Steidl, P. (2014). *Neurobranding* (2nd ed.) CreateSpace. Page 15.

51 Fitzsimons, G. M., Chartrand, T. L., & Fitzsimons, G. J. (2008). Automatic effects of brand exposure on motivated behavior: How Apple makes you "think different." *Journal of Consumer Research*, *35*(1), 21–35.

52 Norton, M. I., Mochon, D., & Ariely, D. (2012). The IKEA effect: When labor leads to love. *Journal of Consumer Psychology*, *22*(3), 453–460; Palmer, M. (Host). (2020, August 7). The IKEA effect and effort heuristic (No. 112) [Audio podcast episode]. In *The Brainy Business*.

53 Dillon, R., Sperling, J., & Tietz, J. (2018, October 29). A small nudge to create stunning team results. *McKinsey Organization Blog*. Retrieved from: mckinsey.com/business-functions/people-and-organizational-performance/our-insights/the-organization-blog/a-small-nudge-to-create-stunning-team-results.

54 Williams, L. E., & Bargh, J. A. (2008). Experiencing physical warmth promotes interpersonal warmth. *Science, 322*(5901), 606–607. This study has not been replicated by others. However, I have still chosen to include the study to show how the literal association within the brain works and get you thinking about how this can impact your business via image and word choice.

55 To learn more about building businesses that scale, I highly recommend listening to episode 190 of *The Brainy Business*, where I interviewed John List on his book, *The voltage effect: How to make good ideas great and great ideas scale*.

56 [TedX Talks]. (February 3, 2015). *Missing what's missing: How survivorship bias skews our perception | David McRaney | TEDxJackson* [Video]. YouTube. youtube.com/watch?v=NtUCxKsK4xg; Palmer, M. (Host). (2020, July 24). Survivorship bias: Are you missing what's missing? (No. 110) [Audio podcast episode]. In *The Brainy Business*; Palmer, M. (Host). (2022, June 24). How minds change, with David McRaney (No. 210) [Audio podcast episode]. In *The Brainy Business*.

57 Palmer, M. (2020, January 7). Why you should overestimate the true value of your products. *Inc*. Retrieved from: www.inc.com/melina-palmer/why-you-should-overestimate-true-value-of-your-products.html.

58 Staff. (2014, October 12). The perks of shopping at high end stores. *Yahoo Style*. Retrieved from: www.yahoo.com/news/the-perks-of-shopping-at-high-end-stores-99504199851.html.

59 Staff. (n.d.). 14 types of social proof and how to use it to drive conversions. *SocialToaster*. Retrieved from: www.socialtoaster.com/social-media-marketing-social-proof-conversions; Bernazzani, S. (2021, February 4). 20 examples of social proof in action in 2021. *Hubspot Blog*. Retrieved from: blog.hubspot.com/marketing/social-proof-examples.

60 Baer, J., & Lemin, D. (2018). *Talk triggers: The complete guide to creating customers with word of mouth*. Portfolio.

61 West, C. (2023, January 9). Micro-influencer marketing guide: Facts and uses. *Sprout Social*. Retrieved from: sproutsocial.com/insights/microinfluencer-marketing.

62 Palmer, M. (Host). (2021, November 12). The power of us, interview with Dominic Packer (refreshed episode) (No. 304) [Audio podcast episode]. In *The Brainy Business*; Van Bavel, J. J., & Packer, D. J. (2021). *The power of us: Harnessing our shared identities to improve performance, increase cooperation, and promote social harmony*. Little, Brown Spark.; Johnson, M., & Ghuman, P. (2020). *Blindsight: The (mostly) hidden ways marketing reshapes our brains*. BenBella Books.; Palmer, M. (Host). (2021, July 8). Neuroscience and psychology in the business world, with Matt Johnson (No. 160) [Audio podcast episode]. In *The Brainy Business*; Palmer, M. (Host). (2021, September 30). Why we like the things we like, with Prince Ghuman (No. 172) [Audio podcast episode]. In *The Brainy Business*.

63 Dooley, R. (2019). *Friction: The untapped force that can be your most powerful advantage*. McGraw-Hill Education.; Palmer, M. (Host). (2023, March 27). Friction, with Roger Dooley (refreshed episode) (No. 274) [Audio podcast episode]. In *The Brainy Business*.

64 Kahneman, D., Fredrickson, B., Schreiber, C., & Redelmeier, D. (1993). When more pain is preferred to less: Adding a better end. *Psychological Science, 4*(6), 401–405.; Palmer, M. (Host). (2020, April 23). Peak-end rule (No. 97) [Audio podcast episode]. In *The Brainy Business*.

65 Pecho, B. (2018, August 30). 25 secrets of the magic kingdom. *Chicago Tribune*. Retrieved from: www.chicagotribune.com/news/ct-xpm-1997-12-07-9712070475-story.html; A special thank-you to Jennifer Clinehens for first introducing me to this case study when she was my guest in episode 141 of *The Brainy Business*.

66 Thomas, A. (2018, February 26). The secret ratio that proves why customer reviews are so important. *Inc*. Retrieved from: www.inc.com/andrew-thomas/the-hidden-ratio-that-could-make-or-break-your-company.html.

67 Palmer, M. (Host). (2023, April 3). Leveraging the power of surprise & delight (refreshed episode) (No. 276) [Audio podcast episode]. In *The Brainy Business*.; Berman, B. (2005). How to delight your customers. *California Management Review, 48*(1), 129–151.

68 Peters, L. (2019, June 5). Ed Sheeran is so obsessed with ketchup that Heinz just named a bottle after him. *Bustle*. Retrieved from: www.bustle.com/p/heinz-ketchup-ed-sheeran-released-edchup-bottles-heres-how-you-can-get-one-17951614.

69 Campbell, A. (2015, April 21). Here's how to get your Pret a Manger coffee for free. *Huffington Post*. Retrieved from: www.huffpost.com/entry/free-pret-coffee_n_7112796.

70 Cialdini, R. B. (2021). *Influence, new and expanded: The psychology of persuasion*. Harper Business; Palmer, M. (Host). (2023, August 8). Influence, and the (now!) 7 principles of persuasion, with Robert Cialdini (refreshed episode) (No. 312) [Audio podcast episode]. In *The Brainy Business*.

71 Palmer, M. (Host). (2023, July 14). For the culture, with Marcus Collins (No. 305) [Audio podcast episode]. In *The Brainy Business; Collins, M. (2023). For the culture: The power behind what we buy, what we do, and who we want to be.* PublicAffairs.

72 Palmer, M. (Host). (2023, June 30). Magic words, with Jonah Berger (No. 301) [Audio podcast episode]. In *The Brainy Business*; Berger, J. (2023). *Magic words: What to say to get your way*. Harper Business.

73 Peck, J. & Shu, S. B. (2009). The effect of mere touch on perceived ownership. *Journal of Consumer Research, 36*(3), 434–434.

74 Pradeep, A.K. (2010). *The buying brain: Secrets for selling to the subconscious mind*. John Wiley & Sons.

75 Ramachandran, V. (2009, November). *The neurons that shaped civilization* [Video]. TED Conferences. www.ted.com/talks/vilayanur_ramachandran_the_neurons_that_shaped_civilization; Palmer, M. (Host). (2019, January 18). Mirror neurons: A fascinating discovery from a monkey, a hot day, and an ice cream cone. (No. 31) [Audio podcast episode]. In *The Brainy Business*.

76 Staff. (n.d.). New Coke: The most memorable marketing blunder ever? *Coca-Cola: About Us*. Retrieved from: www.coca-colacompany.com/about-us/history/new-coke-the-most-memorable-marketing-blunder-ever.

77 The 6 Principles of Persuasion by Dr. Robert Cialdini [official site]. (2019, June 25). Retrieved from: www.influenceatwork.com/principles-of-persuasion.

78 Lynn, M. (2011, March). MegaTips 2: Twenty tested techniques to increase your tips. *The Center for Hospitality Research, 1*(2).

79 Subaru Ambassador [official site]. (n.d.). Retrieved from: www.subaruambassador.com.

80 Dunn, K. (2023, February 27). Branded podcasts: Best 20 of 2023. *Ausha*. Retrieved from: www.ausha.co/blog/branded-podcasts.

81 Tell Me What Happened [official website]. (n.d.). Retrieved from: www.onstar.com/podcast.

82 Weinstein, M. (2022). *The power of scarcity: Leveraging urgency and demand to influence customer decisions*. McGraw Hill.; Palmer, M. (Host). (2023, March 16). The power of scarcity, with Mindy Weinstein (No. 271) [Audio podcast episode]. In *The Brainy Business*.

83 Zellermayer, O. (1996). The pain of paying. (doctoral dissertation). Department of Social and Decision Sciences, Carnegie Mellon University, Pittsburgh, PA.; Palmer, M. (Host).

(2022, November 28). Pain of paying (refreshed episode) (No. 240) [Audio podcast episode]. In *The Brainy Business*.

84 Kahneman, D. (2011). *Thinking, fast and slow*. Farrar, Straus and Giroux.

85 Palmer, M. (Host). (2023, March 30). The illusion of choice, with Richard Shotton (No. 275) [Audio podcast episode]. In *The Brainy Business*; Shotton, R. (2023). *The illusion of choice: 16 ½ psychological biases that influence what we buy*. Harriman House.

86 Staff. (2019, April 24). Are you using these 8 subject line formulas to get your emails opened? *Campaign Monitor*. Retrieved from: www.campaignmonitor.com/blog/email-marketing/subject-line-formulas.

87 Palmer, M. (Host). (2020, June 12). How to ethically influence people: Interview with author Brian Ahearn. (No. 104) [Audio podcast episode]. In *The Brainy Business*.

88 Thaler, R. H., & Sunstein, C. R. (2008). *Nudge: Improving decisions about health, wealth, and happiness*. Penguin Books.; There is also a seven-part series on NUDGES on *The Brainy Business* podcast, episodes 35–41, which can be found at *thebrainybusiness.com/podcast*.

89 Staff. (n.d.). The keys to abandoned cart recovery and reducing lost sales. *Big Commerce*. Retrieved from: www.bigcommerce.com/articles/ecommerce/abandoned-carts.

90 Palmer, M. (Host). (2021, August 5). How businesses can design for behavior change with Amy Bucher. (No. 164) [Audio podcast episode]. In *The Brainy Business*.; Staff. (n.d.). The COM-B model for behavior change. *The Decision Lab*. Retrieved from: thedecisionlab.com/reference-guide/organizational-behavior/the-com-b-model-for-behavior-change.

91 Details provided via direct interview, which you can hear in episode 116 of *The Brainy Business* podcast, also check out his book: Wendel, S. (2020). *Designing for behavior change: Applying psychology and behavioral economics* (2nd Ed). O'Reilly Media.

92 Palmer, M. (Host). (2022, February 24). How to create courses people actually enjoy (and complete!) with Chris Rawlinson of 42courses. (No. 193) [Audio podcast episode]. In *The Brainy Business*.

93 Ahearn, B. (2019), *Influence people: Powerful everyday opportunities to persuade that are lasting and ethical*. Influence People, LLC.; Palmer, M. (Host). (2020, June 12). How to ethically influence people: Interview with author Brian Ahearn. (No. 104) [Audio podcast episode]. In *The Brainy Business*.

94 Lam, B. (2015, January 30). The psychological difference between $12.00 and $11.67. *The Atlantic*.

95 Wadhwa, M. & Zhang, K. (2014). This number just feels right: The impact of roundedness of price numbers on product evaluations. *Journal of Consumer Research, 41*(5), 1172–1185.

96 Palmer, M. (Host). (2018, September 6). Relativity: A behavioral economics foundations episode. (No. 12) [Audio podcast episode]. In *The Brainy Business*.; Palmer, M. (Host). (2020, June 12). How to ethically influence people: Interview with author Brian Ahearn. (No. 104) [Audio podcast episode]. In *The Brainy Business*.

97 Thaler, R. H., Sunstein, C. R., & Balz, J. P. (2012). Choice architecture. The behavioral foundations of public policy, Ch. 25, Eldar Shafir, ed. (2012).

98 Terao, Y., Fukuda, H., & Hikosaka, O. (2017). What do eye movements tell us about patients with neurological disorders?—An introduction to saccade recording in the clinical setting. *Proceedings of the Japan Academy. Series B, Physical and Biological Sciences, 93*(10), 772–801.

99   Zellermayer, O. (1996). The pain of paying. (doctoral dissertation). Department of Social and Decision Sciences, Carnegie Mellon University, Pittsburgh, PA.; Palmer, M. (Host). (2022, November 28). Pain of paying (refreshed episode) (No. 240) [Audio podcast episode]. In *The Brainy Business*.

100 Mack, M. (n.d.). People try world's most expensive grilled cheese. *Buzzfeed*. Retrieved from: www.buzzfeed.com/watch/video/26070.

101 Lane, T. (2023, May 18). How to buy a Birkin bag, according to an expert. *InStyle*. Retrieved from: www.instyle.com/fashion/accessories/bags/how-to-buy-a-birkin-bag; Staff. (2023, July 18). The history of the Hermès Birkin bag and how it became so expensive. *Glam Observer*. Retrieved from: glamobserver.com/the-history-of-the-hermes-birkin-bag-and-how-it-became-so-expensive; Staff. (2020, September 13). Story of a Hermès Birkin: How I got mine, and tips for bagging one. *Happy High Life blog*. Retrieved from: www.happyhighlife.com/hermes-how-to-get-a-birkin.

102 Kuczynski, A. (2004, April 18). NOTICED; On this accessory, the jury isn't out. *The New York Times*. Retrieved from: www.nytimes.com/2004/04/18/style/noticed-on-this-accessory-the-jury-isn-t-out.html.

103 Vegas Dave [@itsvegasdave]. (2019, April 28). Vegas Dave buys record breaking $500,000 Hermès Birkin bag [Instagram video]. Retrieved from: www.instagram.com/p/Bwz7zB0jkrR/?hl=en.

104 Staff. (2014, October 14). The anatomy of a $432,000 handbag. *Vogue*. Retrieved from: www.vogue.com/article/most-expensive-hermes-birkin.

105 Staff. (n.d.). Hermès history and authentication techniques. *Labels Luxury*. Retrieved from: www.labelsluxury.com/pages/hermes.

106 Tungate, M. (2017, November 9). A brief history of Ryanair. *Management Today*. Retrieved from: www.managementtoday.co.uk/brief-history-ryanair/food-for-thought/article/1449458; Boon, T. (2021, November 6). The story of Ryanair: Ireland's LCC used to be anything but low cost. *Simple Flying*. Retrieved from: simpleflying.com/ryanair-history.

107 Old Navy: About Us [official website] (n.d.). Retrieved from: www.gapinc.com/en-us/about/old-navy; Old Navy: History [official website]. (n.d.). Retrieved from: www.gapinc.com/en-us/about/old-navy/old-navy-history.

108 Staff. (2018, April 6). Old Navy sets the bar. *License Global*. Retrieved from: www.licenseglobal.com/beauty-cosmetics/old-navy-sets-bar.

109 Malinsky, G. (2019, June 7). The 'fat tax' is real. Here are 5 examples that prove it's more expensive to be plus-sized. *Business Insider*. Retrieved from: www.businessinsider.com/fat-tax-examples-clothing-fashion-flying-bikes-furniture-coffin-2019-6.

Mango Publishing, established in 2014, publishes an eclectic list of books by diverse authors—both new and established voices—on topics ranging from business, personal growth, women's empowerment, LGBTQ studies, health, and spirituality to history, popular culture, time management, decluttering, lifestyle, mental wellness, aging, and sustainable living. We were recently named 2019 *and* 2020's #1 fastest growing independent publisher by *Publishers Weekly*. Our success is driven by our main goal, which is to publish high-quality books that will entertain readers as well as make a positive difference in their lives.

Our readers are our most important resource; we value your input, suggestions, and ideas. We'd love to hear from you—after all, we are publishing books for you!

Please stay in touch with us and follow us at:

Facebook: Mango Publishing

Twitter: @MangoPublishing

Instagram: @MangoPublishing

LinkedIn: Mango Publishing

Pinterest: Mango Publishing

Newsletter: mangopublishinggroup.com/newsletter

Join us on Mango's journey to reinvent publishing, one book at a time.

Printed in the USA
CPSIA information can be obtained
at www.ICGtesting.com
JSHW030310111223
53531JS00005B/5

9 781684 813438